LOST RAILWAYS
OF
NORTHUMBERLAND

LOST RAILWAYS
OF
NORTHUMBERLAND

Robert Kinghorn

COUNTRYSIDE BOOKS
NEWBURY, BERKSHIRE

First published 2006
© Robert Kinghorn 2006

COUNTRYSIDE BOOKS
3 Catherine Road
Newbury, Berkshire

To view our complete range of books,
please visit us at
www.countrysidebooks.co.uk

ISBN 1 85306 989 9
EAN 978 1 85306 989 5

The cover picture shows Lambley station and viaduct
and is from an original painting by
Colin Doggett

Produced through MRM Associates Ltd., Reading
Typeset by CJWT Solutions, Newton-le-Willows
Printed by Woolnough Bookbinding Ltd., Irthlingborough

CONTENTS

ABBREVIATIONS

BCR	Border Counties Railway
B&TR	Blyth & Tyne Railway
BUR	Border Union Railway
CR	Caledonian Railway
DMU	Diesel Multiple Unit
ECML	East Coast Main Line
EMU	Electric Multiple Unit
GNER	Great North Eastern Railway
GNR	Great Northern Railway
GSWR	Glasgow & South Western Railway
GWR	Great Western Railway
LNER	London & North Eastern Railway
LNR	Leeds Northern Railway
NBR	North British Railway
N&BR	Newcastle & Berwick Railway
NCR	Northumberland Central Railway
N&CR	Newcastle & Carlisle Railway
NER	North Eastern Railway
N&DJR	Newcastle & Darlington Junction Railway
N&NSR	Newcastle & North Shields Railway
NSR	North Sunderland Light Railway
SN&WR	Scotswood, Newburn & Wylam Dock & Railway Company
WVR	Wansbeck Valley Railway
YN&BR	York, Newcastle & Berwick Railway

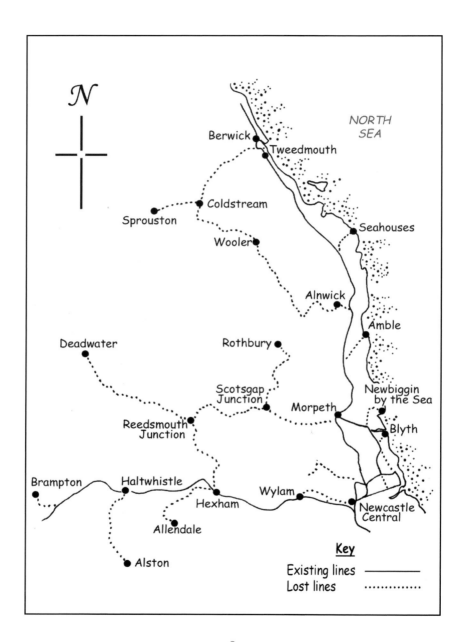

NORTH SEA

N

Berwick
Tweedmouth
Coldstream
Sprouston
Wooler
Seahouses
Alnwick
Amble
Deadwater
Rothbury
Scotsgap Junction
Morpeth
Newbiggin by the Sea
Reedsmouth Junction
Blyth
Brampton
Haltwhistle
Wylam
Hexham
Newcastle Central
Allendale
Alston

<u>Key</u>

Existing lines ——————

Lost lines ·················

Introduction

Walk down Hillheads Road in Whitley Bay, past the ice rink, and on your left just before the supermarket is a public house called The Railway. Which railway? Where was it and from where to where did it run? Here is a mystery to be solved, but how many passers-by notice, or ever wonder where that railway was?

Northumberland was the home and heart of the Industrial Revolution, mainly due to the invention of the steam locomotive by a local man, George Stephenson. It meant that the coal could be transported long distances for use far away from where it was mined. The commerce on the great River Tyne was driven by coal exports and the industries that used coal, and other rivers and coastal ports, such as Blyth, also depended on coal. Yet, although the needs of industry were the origin of Northumberland's rail system, passenger transport became increasingly important over the years and this book sets out to find those passenger lines and stations which came and have gone, but are not forgotten. For the curious, there is a lot to seek and a lot to find of Northumberland's lost railways.

The railway referred to in that public house sign was the Blyth and Tyne (B&TR), originally a mineral line, which ran from near Morpeth, south to the Tyne at Tynemouth and Percy Main. It was one of many in that area taking coal from the pits to the ports, the remains of which can still be seen today. The B&TR was different to the other colliery waggonways, however, as it started carrying passengers and opened a line to New Bridge Street in central Newcastle which became a major passenger route, electrified by the NER and then converted to become part of the Tyne and Wear Metro. The B&TR was eventually swallowed by the regional railway super-power, the North Eastern Railway (NER), which was based at York and ran north to Berwick, east to the coast and as far west as Carlisle.

The NER section of the East Coast Main Line from London Kings Cross to Aberdeen via Edinburgh was an early source of passenger traffic, with many stations serving small communities. Later, local lines such as to Carlisle, Tynemouth or Ponteland, as well as the B&TR, expanded passenger rail traffic. Following the grouping of companies that took place in 1923, in the 1930s the London & North Eastern Railway (LNER) had 119 open passenger stations on 316 miles of railway in Northumberland. By 1992 that had shrunk to 20 stations on 130 route miles. But don't despair, there is a feast of relics waiting to be found if you know what you are looking for and where to look.

Some of these lines are still important, such as the ECML or those now in the guise of the Tyne and Wear Metro, but with many stations now closed or demolished. Other lines have been totally closed. One group includes branches from either the main line or the Tyne Valley line between Newcastle and Carlisle, such as those to Seahouses and Amble from the ECML, or to Allendale and Alston from the Tyne Valley line. Another group of now totally closed lines are those built as a result of the rivalry between the NER and the North British Railway (NBR), which was always trying to get its own access to Newcastle. Likewise, the NER's fear of the NBR was the reason for the lines from Alnmouth to Coldstream and from Berwick to Sprouston Junction, via Coldstream. None now carry passengers or freight but there is still a lot to be found and to excite the railway relics hunter.

Two links with the past are the Stephenson Railway Museum and the North Tyneside Steam Railway, which runs from the museum to Percy Main along the route of one of the old colliery lines. From it can be seen more signs of the many lines that once served the Tyne.

By the early 20th century, the NER had lost nearly a third of its suburban passengers to electric tramways. Their response was electrification of the line from Newcastle Central via Wallsend to Whitley Bay and then back via Gosforth to Newcastle New Bridge Street Station. This included the 6-mile Riverside Branch, the goods only branch to Newcastle quayside and the main line from Benton to Heaton Junction.

This was a major change in railway operation. It was the first third rail (600 volts DC) multiple unit electrified railway in the UK, other than the London Underground and Tube lines. To operate the system, the NER bought a new fleet of radically different trains, a dramatic break with British railway tradition. The trains were painted cream around the windows, with red on the match boarding below the waistline. In all, 39 coaches, 33 trailers and 2 motor luggage vans provided 195 trains a day. They were revolutionary for their time. Gone were the compartments. These were replaced with open saloons, with straw basket-weave covered reversible tram-type seats, two each side of a central gangway. There were clerestory roofs, destination indicators over the driving cabs, vestibules at each end, with gates that were soon replaced with wooden doors, and couplers which did not require buffers.

The NER was duly proud of its new system and stock. Pride comes before a fall, however, and on 11th August 1918 disaster struck in the form of a fire which destroyed both the Walker Gate Carriage Sheds (Heaton Car Sheds) and 34 cars, as well as seriously damaging many others. A replacement depot at Gosforth was opened on 30th September 1923 and new coaches of the same design but with elliptical roofs replaced the destroyed cars. In 1937, the LNER bought new steel 2-car articulated units and, in 1955, BR provided some Eastleigh-built, 2-car EMUs. The seating was 3, plus 2, giving 10 people per bay, and each bay had its own doors. On most

11

The NER lamp at Norham station in 2005. (Author)

of the electrified system, 8 car units were used but because of short platforms on the Riverside Branch 6 car units were used.

Experimental services started between Carville and Percy Main on the Riverside branch on 27th September 1903, the anniversary of the opening of the Stockton and Darlington Railway in 1825. At 12.50 pm, on Tuesday 29th March 1904, electric passenger services started from New Bridge Street to Benton. The service train had been preceded at 12.05 pm by a Special, carrying NER officers and invited guests.

In the 1950s, so many mothers, with prams, were using the train to visit the coast that four parcel vans were converted to pram vans, with seats for the mothers, and marshalled in with the electric units. In 1963, BR replaced the electric trains south of the Tyne with diesel multiple units (DMUs) and, in 1967, replaced the electric units on the lines north of the Tyne with DMUs. The last electric train left Central Station at 6.15 pm on 17th June 1967.

Disused railway lines are marvellous corridors of undisturbed countryside and wild flowers, such as wild pansies, vetches and ragwort, akin to those in surrounding agricultural land, thrive. Many, however, were brought by the railway, their seeds being carried along by the rolling stock. Others, such as rose bay willow herb, also known as fireweed (everywhere along the trackbed in summer!) thrived on the railway because the frequent burning of the embankments, either accidentally from falling coals or deliberately to control the vegetation, promoted a nitrate-rich soil. Near stations and villages are garden escapees – fruit bushes and trees, as well as flowers. Many railwaymen were keen gardeners, as the remains of their gardens testify, with lupins, roses and irises being common, together with rhubarb, raspberries and currant bushes. Shade-loving plants such as ferns can be found in cuttings and under bridges, and the ground should be closely scrutinised for the smaller plants. Please remember to respect the Country Code – do not disturb wildlife and never pick or uproot the plants.

Ordnance Survey map references for the lost stations and other points of interest are provided, wherever possible, because some relics, such as the first Cullercoats station on the B&TR, are now hidden forever in the midst of housing or industrial estates or retail parks. Please remember that, apart from those areas converted into public paths, the land is private and some of the surviving station buildings are people's houses. Please respect their privacy. Always obtain permission before entering someone else's land, never damage their property or the wildlife, keep dogs under control, leave no litter and always close gates behind you. Some of the sites described in this book are still in railway use and therefore dangerous. Most of what is mentioned, however, can be seen from the public highway so it is not necessary to trespass or risk your life.

There is a lot to discover. It's time to go hunting!

Robert Kinghorn

1

The Tyne Valley Branches

Newcastle to Scotswood
The Scotswood, Newburn & Wylam Dock
& Railway Company
The Allendale Branch
The Alston Branch

We forget how difficult travel was before the railways. The Tyne Valley was the shortest route coast-to-coast, but the only way to cross it was by walking. The very rich rode or travelled by coach, but horses were mainly used to pull wagons with goods. The poor state of the roads meant that commercial transport was as limited as private travel.

In 1829 George Stephenson, the 'Father of Railways', surveyed a route between Newcastle and Carlisle and, in 1835, the first section of railway track between Blaydon and Hexham was opened. By 1839, the line was open between Carlisle and Redheugh in Gateshead. From this line several branches were constructed, none of which now exist.

When it opened, the Newcastle & Carlisle Railway (N&CR) was the longest in Britain, and the first east to west across England. It also ran on the right, rather than on the left as now. Today, a short stub of the N&CR north of the Tyne, visible from Redheugh Road Bridge, remains open, but the rest of the N&CR line north of the Tyne was closed in 1966 and the tracks were removed in 1972, with part of the route turned into a public bridleway. The N&CR from Newcastle is now accessed from south of the river joining the N&CR at

Blaydon, just west of the line over the disused bridge from Scotswood. Not all has been lost, however, and many old railway items await discovery.

Newcastle to Scotswood

Ask where the station in Newcastle is today and everyone will direct you to Central station. Ask about others and they will probably suggest various Metro stations. Imagine discovering a railway terminus within five minutes' walk of Central station that is unknown to most people in present-day bustling Newcastle!

Halfway down Forth Bank, at the junction with Pottery Lane, is Forth Bank station (NZ 246636), a large yellow building with a neo-classical façade, the terminus of the line from Carlisle that has not seen a passenger train since 1851.

Forth Bank station today – it has not seen a passenger train since 1851. (Author)

16

The platforms were on the second floor, with open arches into the train shed, which had a pitched glazed roof supported by iron trusses. The line ran alongside Pottery Lane over brick arches from Shot Tower station.

The 1906 line from Central station to King Edward Bridge crossed the tracks and platforms of Forth Bank, limiting its use. The N&CR station and walls are in yellow sandstone, while the East Coast Main Line (ECML) to the bridge is in red sandstone. Good views can be obtained from where King Edward Bridge crosses Pottery Lane, and from trains on the bridge. Forth Bank station covered a much larger area before the King Edward Bridge and Kings House (dated 1903) were built as, after 1851, Forth Bank became not just a goods depot, but one of the largest in Europe.

The first N&CR terminus north of the river, Shot Tower, was just north of the car and coach park of the Metro Radio

Forth goods station in the 1930s, when it was one of the largest goods depots in Europe. (Newcastle City Library)

17

Centre. Through the heavy hedge of small trees can be seen what could be the remains of a platform. The bridge that took this line to Forth Bank station has a Network Rail notice reading: 'Frog/3 Redheugh Bridge Road/Shot Factory'. Further north up Redheugh Bridge Road the line to Central station crosses, albeit much higher as it is rising to the station.

Elswick (NZ 221634) was the first station west and was used by workers from the huge Scotswood Road Vickers factories founded by Sir W. G. Armstrong, later Lord Armstrong of Cragside (1810-1900). It is said that locals could not sleep due to the noise from this complex. The station had a 25 ft-wide island platform, with a glazed canopy, supported on brackets incorporating the Star of David. From September 1961 it became an unstaffed halt before closing in January 1967. Here were sidings for Jobling Purser's pitch factory at Paradise Works. The A695 has been widened and straightened into a dual carriageway, removing most traces of the station except pieces of walling.

West of Elswick the railway line has become the North Tyne Cycleway and the Tyne Riverside Country Park, and the route can easily be followed to Wylam Bridge.

The next station was Scotswood (NZ 200639), where the original 1839 N&CR line crossed the river to Blaydon. In 1875, the Scotswood, Newburn and Wylam Dock and Railway Company (SN&WR) opened a line along the north bank of the Tyne to Wylam (see below), where it crossed the river to join the N&CR. Immediately west of the junction was Scotswood station, which had four platforms, two for the line across the Tyne to Blaydon and two for the SN&WR. The original station burned down in October 1879 and when replaced had both a footbridge and a subway to connect them.

By 1967 all the platforms had closed and, sadly, very few traces of the line or station remain. North of the Scotswood road bridge can be seen the retaining walls for the line and a cast-iron over-bridge. Not far west, however, we are in for a great delight as we find another major part of the N&CR – the embankment to the bridge to Blaydon, which can be seen from the river's edge (turn left at the next traffic lights, signed to the right to B&Q).

The Scotswood, Newburn and Wylam Dock and Railway Company

The SN&WR's line along the north bank of the River Tyne, opened in July 1875 and followed most of the route of the Wylam Waggonway from North Wylam to Scotswood. Wylam railway bridge over the River Tyne, joining the SN&WR to the N&CR line, opened the following year. The SN&WR was taken over by the North Eastern Railway (NER) in 1883.

Lemington station (NZ 188647) had a brick stationmaster's

Trams and buses took passengers away from Lemington station, seen here in the 1920s. (Newcastle City Libraries)

19

house and wooden buildings on each platform, but trams and buses took away its trade and it closed to passengers in September 1958, to general goods in January 1960 and to coal in July 1963. The station, now a private house, is clearly visible from the cycleway.

Between Lemington and the next station of Newburn we are again cheered by finding a major artefact of the SN&WR, the large metal bridge where the track and now the cycleway crosses the road. There is nothing left of Newburn station (NZ 164654), which had several wooden buildings on the up (Newcastle) platform, a single one on the down, a wooden footbridge on brick pillars and an NER signal box at the crossing. The station closed to passengers in September 1958 and to goods in April 1965.

Prior to the arrival of the railway at Heddon-on-the-Wall

Newburn station, on Grange Road – only the bridge survives. (Newcastle City Libraries)

Before the opening of Heddon-on-the-Wall station, the ferry to Ryton station across the Tyne was the only option for locals wanting to travel. (Stations UK)

(NZ 145656) in July 1885, locals wanting to travel had to walk to the riverbank and catch the ferry across the Tyne to Ryton station; in 1877 three residents of Heddon had lost their lives in a ferry accident. The area has hosted a wide variety of industries, including salmon fishing on the River Tyne, coalmining, the quarrying of sandstone and limestone, brickmaking and, of course, agriculture. Heddon-on-the-Wall station was about ¾ mile along the road from the village and about 400 ft lower. It opened in July 1881 but was completely closed in September 1958 with the buildings, typical NER wooden booking office and waiting rooms, being demolished in 1959. Today nothing can be seen other than the cycleway and a house called Station House.

The last SN&WR station was North Wylam (NZ 119648), with single-storey brick buildings containing booking and parcels offices, as well as general and ladies' waiting rooms, with a signal box at the east end. By the 1960s, staff from Wylam station, across the road bridge over the Tyne, would walk over the bridge, sell tickets to any North Wylam passengers, and do the accounts. The rest of the day the porter sold the tickets. North Wylam station was nearer the village and thus handier for passengers but, as fewer trains ran on this line, the other station was far busier. Goods ceased to be handled in January 1961 and passengers last alighted in March 1965. Sadly, this is another station that has completely disappeared, except for the edge of a platform in the car park. One of the gang employed to flatten the station remembers thinking what a waste it was, but he needed the job!

The Newcastle *Courant* of 17th January 1874 reported: 'Wylam is the very worst colliery village that we have yet beheld.' Besides the thriving colliery and ironworks, a leadshot works and a brewery were all established in the village. Wylam has also an important place in the development of locomotives and the railways. The Railway Museum opened in 1981 in the old village school, now known as the Falcon Centre in Falcon Terrace. Its opening celebrated the bicentenary of the birth of George Stephenson and commemorated Wylam's unique contribution to railway history.

One of the earliest waggonways opened in 1748 between Wylam Colliery and the staiths at Lemington and, in 1804, Richard Trevithick built a locomotive, *Wylam*, to replace the horse-drawn coal waggons. At five tons, it was too heavy for the wooden waggonway.

George Stephenson was born in Wylam in June 1781, at a small cottage (NZ 127650) called Street House, which may still be visited. It is about ½ mile eastwards along the trackbed path from the car park on the site of North Wylam station. At twelve years of age George was tending cows for 2d a day and he did not learn to read until he was 19. When he worked at the same pit as his father, his interest in and ability with

The cottage where George Stephenson, 'Father of the Railways', was born in 1781 at Wylam. (Author)

machinery meant that by 1798 he was in charge of the pumping engines at Water Row Pit in Newburn, and then brakesman at Killington where his skills earned him the nickname of 'engine doctor'.

Others remembered at the museum include Timothy Hackworth, whose father was foreman blacksmith at the colliery and who was born in the village in December 1786. Hackworth, William Hedley (the Wylam Colliery manager) and Jonathan Forster developed the locomotive engines at the colliery, the most famous of which was *Puffing Billy*, now at the Science Museum in London. The wonderfully evocative items of local railwayana, old photographs, posters and models at Wylam, many collected by local enthusiasts, will keep you there a long time.

Wylam railway bridge (Author)

About ½ mile west of North Wylam is yet another superb discovery. At Hagg Bank the line and footpath crossed Wylam railway bridge (NZ 111643). Opened in 1876, it allowed N&CR trains to cross the River Tyne and join the SN&WR to Newcastle. The wrought-iron bridge has an 80 yard arch from which the deck is suspended from vertical ties. Believed to have been the first of its kind in the world, it is claimed that it was the inspiration for Australia's Sydney Harbour Bridge.

The Allendale Branch

Do you fancy a cup of tea and home-made cakes at an idyllic Victorian railway station? You can enjoy them at the Leaning Shed Café at Langley station, on the Allendale Branch.

The Hexham & Allendale Railway was a 13½ mile single track line originally constructed for the transportation of lead ore from the mines in upland Northumberland to Hexham and on to Newcastle upon Tyne. It opened up to Langley in August 1867 and to Catton Road in January 1868, but passenger facilities were not completed until March 1869 owing to a lack of funds. The services were operated by the NER, which took over the line in July 1876. Passenger services were withdrawn in September 1930 but the end of the goods service and total closure of the line was not until November 1950.

The branch left the N&CR west of Hexham at the Border Counties junction (NZ 921653), where the northbound NBR also branched off. After the junction, the branch curved south-west and climbed steeply into the hills. After 6¼ miles Elrington (NY 862633), a single platform station with two sidings, was the first stop. A lack of passengers meant it became a halt in September 1926. The stone two-storey stationmaster's house, at right angles to the tracks with a lean-to onto the platform that contained the booking office, is now a private house. From the road over-bridge the remains of a cattle dock can be seen, as can the clear trackbed, in a cutting to the south-west.

The line continued curving south-west and climbed 650 ft over 8¾ miles to the summit of the line at Langley (NY 829613), which opened for freight in August 1867. A ground frame controlled the line to Langley smelt mill (NY 830613), fed by the railway from the mines further along the line. In the 19th century the small town of Allendale, 800 ft above sea level, had expanded to become a very prosperous lead mining centre due to extensive mining at Allenheads, the source of the Allen 7 miles south of Allendale, and many other locations in the dale. Smelting took place at Allen Mill and Langley, where large flues were constructed underground to direct fumes to chimneys miles away on the fell top. The lead, which solidified on the walls of the flues as

25

The Allendale-Hexham train pulling into Langley station, c1900. (Jane Torday)

the fumes cooled, could be scraped off and collected for the rail journey to the coast. Now, what little remains is covered by ivy, willowherb and heather.

When the station opened to passengers in March 1869, a band played and the place was festooned with flags. It had two platforms, with a stationmaster's house next to the up platform. Passengers were dealt with on the up platform and a wooden waiting room with central sliding door was provided. The down platform dealt with goods traffic. In July 1936, six years after the last passenger had been carried, the station became Langley-on-Tyne.

This is where we stop for tea and cakes! This delightful site and buildings have become The Garden Station (www.thegardenstation.co.uk), one of the locality's historic visitor attractions. Both platforms survive, now as part of the garden, complete with wooden red toy engine, which occupies what was the trackbed. The Leaning Shed Café is self-service with an honesty box for tea, coffee and home-made cakes during the summer, while over summer weekends and bank holidays the station building is open for the china service of refreshments. In addition, there are plants for sale and a programme of courses and exhibitions that might include gardening, willow weaving, botanical painting and sculpture. The whole location is a brilliant, beautiful and heavenly oasis. This is a 'must call' station.

By January 1868 the line was opened all the way to Allendale, or Catton Road (NY 832569) as it was known until May 1898, via another station at Staward Halt (NY 806597), which had a single platform and a passing loop. In April 1939, nine years after its last passenger, the station became simply Staward.

Staward had a stone-built, two-storey station house, part rendered, with wooden station offices which are now a private residence, and in very good condition. Apart from the grassed trackbed and a large pine where the tracks used to be, it must look very much as it did when trains were running,

It is possible to imagine at Staward how the line would have looked in its heyday. (Ken Hoole Collection)

possibly even better as it is so well kept. Half close your eyes, and you almost feel, hear, smell and see a train as it leaves. Fragments of a coal depot remain, as does an impressive retaining wall for the presumed realignment of the roads when the line was built – the track apart, this is the only significant piece of civil engineering on the line.

Allendale station was designed as a through station with one passenger platform and a 42-ft turntable, with coal cells on the east, while on the west were three sidings, the middle one serving a small goods shed. Despite being the terminus there was no signal box at Allendale and the points were operated by two ground frames. The station house, which was of stone against the platform and, at one stage, had a glazed canopy, remains as the headquarters and office of the Allendale Caravan Park. Also surviving are the platform, a buffer stop, a wooden goods shed and the base of a crane. Again, very little imagination is required for the mind's eye to

Allendale was a prosperous lead mining centre in the 19th century and the station attracted a great deal of traffic. (Stations UK)

see this in its heyday. The town was about a mile from Catton Road station and the station yard was often busy with six to eight horse-drawn vehicles carrying people along Station Road into Allendale.

Allendale's lead boom was relatively shortlived and by the last quarter of the 19th century the industry had declined and the population of the dale fell sharply. By the late 1920s trade on the line had collapsed. Total income was only £1,685 but it cost £4,687 to run the line. It was no surprise when closure came in 1930.

The Alston Branch

Do you want to ride on a steam train on a Northumbrian branch line closed by British Rail? You do? Then this is the line where you can live your dreams.

When news came in 1846 that Royal Assent had been given for the Haltwhistle to Alston branch line (on the N&CR) there was great rejoicing locally. A contemporary account of the news said the whole district of Alston Moor was illuminated, 'and, to wind up the climax, figures in effigy, intended to represent certain oppositionists, were publicly burned by the people'.

Two hundred years ago, Alston was the commercial centre of an important lead mining area, producing about 10,000 tonnes of lead per year and, like the Allendale Branch, the Alston Branch was a 13½ mile single track line built to capture the mineral traffic. Despite the rejoicing, things did not proceed smoothly or quickly. The 1846 Act allowed the extension of the N&CR to Central station in Newcastle and the building of the Nenthead branch, as it was then known, but no work was undertaken. In 1849 a

Haltwhistle, showing the Alston train, in 1957. (R.K. Blencowe)

Haltwhistle, in 1975, with the branch line viaduct seen in the distance on the right. (R.K. Blencowe)

second act allowed the N&CR to abandon the line beyond Alston and take a new route from the east end of Haltwhistle station (NY 704638).

After the Carlisle-facing junction, the line immediately rose on a gradient of 1 in 80 and curved south to cross the River South Tyne on the impressive Alston Arches viaduct (NY 709637), which was built from faced stone with six long and low arches, four of which span the river. It is now a Grade II listed building.

Less than a mile from Haltwhistle was the sometime Penmeller Halt. This 33-yard earth and sleeper platform opened in 1919 for Penmeller Colliery, but closed in 1932. During the Second World War it reopened to service a Ministry of Supplies depot.

Featherstone Park station (NY 682608) was reached after about 3 miles. It had a single platform with a level crossing, controlled by a signal box at the southern end, and sidings incorporating a run-round loop for the inclined tramway connecting it to the nearby colliery. Goods traffic ceased in 1954 but passenger traffic continued until the closure of the branch. All still exists, with the two-storey stone house now a private dwelling and the South Tynedale Trail passing along the trackbed in front of the platform. The station was opened for Featherstone Castle, the oldest part of which is 14th-century. When the late Queen Mother visited Ridley Hall near Bardon Mill, the Royal Train was stabled overnight at Featherstone Park. It was supposed to be a secret but all the locals knew.

A railway passenger would next have come to Coanwood (NY 678590). This was originally named Shaft Hill and closed in May 1853, to reopen as Shafthill in 1862 until 1885 when it

The level crossing at Featherstone Park in 1975. The station building is now a private house and the South Tynedale Trail passes along the track-bed. (R.K. Blencowe)

became Coanwood. Although it had a passing loop, this was for a colliery and whinstone quarry which provided freight traffic for this station and it only boasted a single platform to the east of the loop, again with a level crossing south of it. The platform had a wooden building containing a booking office and waiting room but these were demolished in the 1960s. A second, smaller hut sufficed after that. There was an NER signal box and, well back from the platform, the stationmaster's house. Freight traffic ceased in 1955. At the level crossing site a gate (with concrete gateposts) still remains. To the north, along the South Tynedale Trail, can be seen the old platform and its retaining wall. In the gloomy cutting one can easily imagine a train passing through here on a wet and windy night.

Lambley (NY 674581) was a stone-built station, including a stationmaster's house, while a wooden building for a waiting room was added in the 1890s. The station was on a sharp curve and the inner rail was fitted with a continuous check rail. As there was no room for a passing loop, freight had to be shunted into the branch to the colliery. Goods ceased to be handled here after September 1960. Between the viaduct to the north and the station was the junction to Lambley Colliery and Lord Carlisle's Railway to Brampton, on which George Stephenson's famous *Rocket* ended its working life.

Lambley viaduct (NY 675583) still stands, a very graceful structure and a Grade II listed building, owned by the North Pennines Heritage Trust. It is stone-built, with a 12 ft wide deck about 853 ft long, with nine 58 ft span arches and eight 20 ft spans at 110 ft above the River South Tyne. Three of the pillars supporting the 58 ft arches stand in the water. In 1996 the Lambley viaduct reopened after restoration as a footpath.

The station was reached by a gravel path and is now a private residence. Because of this, the South Tynedale Trail leaves the trackbed to skirt Lambley station and crosses the branch to Lambton Colliery and Lord Carlisle's Railway.

Lambley station, showing the sharp curve of the track. (Lens of Sutton)

Here it descends a flight of rough steps before leading to iron steps up to the viaduct, which the South Tynedale Trail uses at this point to cross the valley. Along the A698 to the next station is a side road affording good, though distant, views of the station and viaduct.

Between Lambley and Slaggyford, an 1880s' resident of one of the trackside cottages had a dog called Hell. This dog waited by the line to pick up and take to his master the newspaper that an obliging guard daily threw from a passing train.

Slaggyford (NY 676524), like the other stations on the branch, had a single platform, with a wooden booking office and two waiting rooms, with a level crossing immediately north of the platform, worked from a brick NER signal box on the west of the track. Again, the loop was not for passing trains but, for operational reasons, connected with the

The platform at Slaggyford is still in good repair, seen here in 1975.
(R.K. Blencowe)

sidings, loading dock, goods shed and, from 1916, the
Anthracite Coal and Lime Company's siding. Passengers
continued to be able to use Slaggyford station until the
closure of the branch but goods services ceased here in
September 1955.

The station house was separate from the platform on the
east of the line. Here a treat awaits you. The station house is
now a private home and nicely looked after with a BR NE
Region nameboard. The platform is in good repair, with the
green and white painted wooden booking office and waiting
room still on it. The trackbed is part of the South Tynedale
Trail, and the South Tynedale Railway has been authorised to
extend to here, although this will entail major restoration
work on the Lintley viaduct, a little over a mile south, as well
as other engineering works. At present, the South Tynedale

District Council is investigating the possibility of rebuilding the railway north from Slaggyford to Haltwhistle alongside the South Tynedale Way.

After this comes a section of steep climbing, at 1 in 56 for a mile. A number of viaducts cross the Lort Burn and the Gilderdale Burn (where the line crossed into what is nowadays Cumbria) and then the South Tyne before Alston station (NY 717467), 875 ft above sea level, was reached, just over 13 miles from and 540 ft higher than Haltwhistle. Alston station had a handsome stone building, with a canopy over the tracks and a built-in stationmaster's house. There were extensive facilities for passengers, goods and cattle. Goods services stopped in September 1965.

Work on the branch progressed slowly and it was not until March 1851 that the 4¼ mile section from Haltwhistle to Shafthill (later Coanwood) opened for freight, with passengers being accommodated from July. In January 1852

Alston Railway Station. 3865

Alston station was once a hive of activity. (Lens of Sutton)

37

Alston station still echoes to the sound and smell of steam trains, as the South Tynedale Preservation Society opened the South Tynedale Railway from here in 1983. (Author)

the 9-mile section from Alston to Lambley was opened. Between then and the completion of the Lambley viaduct, and the opening of the line throughout, on 17 November 1852, passengers were required to walk over the scaffolding to join the connecting trains.

Sufficient land was taken for double track, with the exception of the Lambley viaduct which only accommodated a single line, but this was never required and the line remained single track to the end of its 124 years of service. One man used the Lambley viaduct as a short cut but was convinced it was not a good idea after being caught on the narrow bridge by a train. He only escaped by climbing on the parapet, 100 ft above the valley floor! Other viaducts on the line were wide enough for two tracks, which was a good thing when a train was thrown off the rails in March 1948. No other serious accidents seem to have occurred, but one morning the crew for the first train from Alston found the engine, on its wheels, in the river. The brakes had eased off overnight and there had been just enough steam for it to escape from the engine shed and flatten the buffers that stood in its way before taking an early morning dip.

In the 1930s the LNER introduced Camping Coaches and one was stationed at Alston. It was a former GNR six-wheel coach with some partitions removed to give a living/dining room, complete with cupboards, sink and primus stoves. Two compartments were fitted with bunks as the sleeping accommodation. For £2 10s a week, six people could stay there and be provided with towels, bed linen and cutlery. The nearby station had to be visited for water and toilets. Originally varnished teak, the coach was soon repainted in the LNER's green and cream tourist livery. It was parked in a quiet location by the river.

Freight traffic kept the line going until the 1950s, but in 1955, after the closure of Lambley Colliery, the goods service was withdrawn from Coanwood and intermediate stations become unstaffed halts. In 1959 Diesel Multiple Units (DMUs) ran on the branch but failed to increase traffic, partly due to an inappropriate timetable. In September that year Alston engine shed closed and in 1960 the goods service from Lambley and Slaggyford was withdrawn. At Featherstone Park goods traffic lasted until 1963, and until 1966 at Alston. By 1965 Beeching was recommending the closure of the line, but it was reprieved as there was no all-weather road to Alston. In 1967 Alston station's over-all roof was removed. The last train was seen away from Alston on 1 May 1976 by a pair of pipers and to the thunder of detonators. The line closed two days later.

Don't despair; this is where you can get your ride on a steam train. Alston station still echoes to the sound of iron wheel on iron rail and is pungent with the smell of steam and coal. South Tynedale Railway Preservation Society (www.strps.org.uk) was formed in 1973, later becoming caretaker of England's highest narrow gauge railway. Although unable to save the original standard gauge line, the first mile of a 2 ft-gauge narrow-gauge line northwards from Alston to Gilderdale was opened in July 1983 as the South Tynedale Railway.

The line reached Gilderdale Halt (NY 704485) on the Northumberland border 1½ miles from Alston in December 1986. After substantial work on the viaduct crossing the Lort Burn, a further ¾ mile of track to Kirkhaugh (NY 697497) was opened in Northumberland in September 1999 and it is hoped to extend the line by another 2¼ miles from Kirkhaugh to Slaggyford, which has road access, when the costs of track materials, viaduct work and the renovation of Slaggyford station building and platform can be afforded. Kirkhaugh will then become the mid-point of the line and with its already existing run-round loop, will enable the railway to run two trains, one from each terminus, passing there.

Meanwhile, the society has developed a full range of facilities, including an engine shed, carriage works and shed, and an operating signal box (from Ainderby on the NER line to Redmire) re-erected on a new brick base. It controls all train movements at Alston as well as the lifting barriers (from How Mill station) across the road to the free car and coach park. Alston station has a gift shop and a café. The railway has sixteen steam and diesel locomotives and eight passenger coaches, as well as a large number of works vehicles for maintaining and extending the line. It operates from March to the end of October, with Santa Specials at Christmas.

Near the station in Alston, which claims to be the highest market town in England, are a couple of transport-related exhibitions. One is the Hub, an exhibition of transport memorabilia and related artefacts, housed in the restored

Alston goods shed building, which is located opposite the station. The other, also in Station Yard, is the Alston Model Railway Exhibition Centre, which has a permanent exhibition of at least five model railway layouts in a variety of gauges and is associated with Townfoot Models, a well stocked model shop selling new and secondhand model railway items, tools and materials.

The fascinating history of the lead mining that brought both the Alston and Allendale branches to the area may be further explored by visiting the Nenthead Mines Heritage Centre or the Killhope Lead Mining Museum in Weardale.

2
The Suburban Branches

Ponteland and Darras Hall
Newcastle and Tynemouth Termini
of the N&NSR
The Riverside Branch
The Quayside Branch

Ponteland and Darras Hall

The 1903 NER electrification scheme originally included the proposed 7-mile Gosforth & Ponteland Light Railway, but in

South Gosforth, where the Ponteland Branch left the Blyth & Tyne Railway. (Stations UK)

42

Wed 7th Laguna MOT

Thurs 22nd Honda MOT.

GRANGETOWN AUTO CENTRE

RELIABLE SERVICE FOR ALL MAKES AND MODELS

CLASS 4, 5 & 7 MOT TEST STATION AND REPAIR CENTRE

TONY HEPPLE

RYHOPE ROAD
SUNDERLAND
SR2 0SP

0191 5239666 / 07778750999
0191 5239689
TONYHEPPLE@HOTMAIL.CO.UK

• GRANGETOWN AUTO CENTRE •

fact the line was steam-operated from its opening in June 1905 until it closed to passengers in June 1929. Freight continued to be carried until after the Second World War and then, in the 1960s, electric stock awaiting scrapping was stored on the branch. The section from South Gosforth to Bank Foot became part of the electrified Metro and was later extended to Newcastle airport on a diversion from the original line. Today, the trackbed from the point of diversion to Ponteland is a bridleway.

The Ponteland Branch left the Blyth & Tyne Railway (B&TR) at South Gosforth (NZ 252680) and turned north-west to West Gosforth station (NZ 243687), which originally had attractive wooden single-storey NER buildings. A time traveller would not recognise it now, as it has been totally rebuilt as Regent Centre Metro with nothing remaining of the original. Likewise, sadly, there is no trace of Coxlodge station

West Gosforth Station.

West Gosforth station, which has been completely rebuilt as Regent Centre Metro. (Lens of Sutton)

43

There is now no trace of the original Coxlodge station, rebuilt as Fawdon Metro. (Stations UK)

(NZ 229689), which had single-storey wooden buildings on both platforms and a low brick signal box. On the site is now Fawdon Metro station.

Kenton (NZ 207688) was renamed by the LNER as Kenton Bank in July 1923, in case anyone got confused with the Suffolk station of Kenton! It had a single platform, graced with a standard wooden building, a passing loop and a signal box. Once again, our time traveller would not recognise the totally rebuilt station now known as Bankfoot Metro, nor the next one, Callerton (NZ 190704).

Ponteland (NZ 163729) was a single-platform station with a larger version of the branch's standard single-storey wooden building, but with a glazed canopy. The site is now the Merton Way Shopping Area and the sole remains, a row of houses called 'Station Cottages', are on the Ponteland Industrial Estate, which occupies what were the goods sidings.

Kenton station, renamed Kenton Bank in 1923 in case anyone thought they were in Suffolk! (Lens of Sutton)

Ponteland station, shown here in 1830, now lies beneath the Merton Way shopping centre. (Stations UK)

45

When Royalty visiting the North East were using the Royal Train, this branch was an ideal overnight place of rest. HM King George V and HM Queen Mary spent the night at Ponteland station on 9th October 1928. The train comprised eleven coaches and two locomotives, to keep it heated, plus an accumulator van for electrical power. A row of suburban coaches provided a screen from the nearby cottages!

A Garden City for professionals and managers, a Shangri La away from the bustle of Newcastle, was the aim of the 1907 Darras Hall Estate developers. To serve this oasis of tranquillity, the Darras Hall Light Railway opened in 1913 and lasted as long as the Ponteland line. However, the line went past Darras Hall to Kirkeaton Colliery and passenger services for the miners were provided from 1921 to 1929. Freight continued until August 1954. From a junction just outside Ponteland station, the light railway ran southwest and almost straight to Darras Hall. It is now a bridleway.

Darras Hall station (NZ 152714) was in the Broadway,

Darras Hall station was more elaborately decorated than others, as part of the vision of the Darras Hall Estate developers in 1907. (Ken Hoole Collection).

where now there is a turning, signposted: 'Station Cottages leading to Old Station Court'. This station was a version of those found on the Ponteland branch but was more elaborately decorated because of its location. Again, nothing remains of the station and on the site now stands a modern United Reformed Church building.

Newcastle and Tynemouth Termini of the N&NSR

One of the earliest lines in the North East, the Newcastle and North Shields Railway (N&NSR), opened in June 1839 from Carliol Square in Newcastle to North Shields. Its promoters hoped it would be an extension of the Newcastle & Carlisle Railway (N&CR), but it soon became part of the York, Newcastle & Berwick Railway (YN&BR) and extended south to what was to become Newcastle Central station. The N&NSR was later extended at its eastern end to a new terminus at Tynemouth, which opened in March 1847.

The N&NSR route to North Shields, with the exception of the two termini, was electrified by the NER in 1904 on the third rail system as part of the coastal loop. It is now part of the Tyne and Wear Metro, using overhead electrification.

Carliol Square (NZ 252642) is one of the great disappointments for railway enthusiasts. All has been swept away. The N&NSR had originally planned a terminus in Pilgrim Street, but services started from a small terminus (NZ 251642) between the south side of Carliol Square (the centre of which contained a prison) and Railway Bank. From its opening in July 1847 to August 1850, the Newcastle and Berwick Railway also used Carliol Square station and the N&NSR line to Heaton Junction (NZ 274654). Then, after the line had been extended south to Central station, the Pilgrim Street terminus was forgotten and Carliol Square closed to passengers in August 1850. Manors station, which had opened in July 1847, catered for those passengers who had found Carliol Square more convenient than Central station.

The construction of the central motorway, which cuts diagonally across Carliol Square from northeast to southwest, and office redevelopment in the 1960s, ensured that nothing now, sadly, remains of this original station.

The other N&NSR terminus was originally at North Shields, but the extension to Tynemouth's first station (NZ 368691) came in 1847. It continued in use for passengers until July 1882 when the NER built their coast line through the new stations at Whitley Bay, Cullercoats and Tynemouth, under the Tynemouth Road, to link with the N&NSR just east of the 1847 terminus. It was used for freight until March 1959.

Situated in Oxford Street, a side street off Tynemouth Road, the 1847 station is a handsome Tudor-style stone building

The 1847 station, terminus for the N&NSR in Oxford Street, Tynemouth, now Grade II listed. (Author)

Tynemouth station in about 1880. (Newcastle City Libraries)

across the ends of the tracks. In the 1990s the platforms were demolished and sheltered housing built on the site, into which the 1847 building, now Grade II listed, has cleverly and sympathetically been incorporated. Originally the station had one 475 ft platform, a shorter bay, two carriage sidings and extensive goods sidings on the southern side.

There was also a line from the western end of the yard past the south-west corner of Collingwood Terrace and then through a valley between Front Street and the Collingwood Monument to, and along, the North Pier of the Tyne. Built for the construction of the North Pier, it went via a blockyard where large blocks of stone were cut to size and shape, and had an engine shed for the line's locomotive. The Tynemouth Volunteer Life Brigade, the first organisation of its sort in the country, had a van on that line.

The line from the blockyard to the station closed in 1882, but parts of the branch can still be seen and the road to Life Brigade House passes over the trackbed. Sections of rusty track can be found on the North Pier.

The Riverside Branch

The 6½ mile Riverside Branch was a southern loop off the N&NSR that opened in May 1879. Between Manors and Percy Main, the Riverside line was 2 miles, or 11 minutes, longer than the direct route. All five original stations were similar with two platforms, one of which held a brick, single-storey main building with a canopy supported by columns between the end pavilions, while the other had smaller brick shelters.

By the 1960s only a limited peak period service for the shipyards remained and that ceased in July 1973. When the Tyneside lines were converted to the Metro system this line was excluded, despite the fact that it would have aided urban regeneration of the area. Here we have a real challenge, but a rewarding one nonetheless. Relics take some finding and none of the stations survive. In some areas all traces of the branch have been obliterated, but in other locations there is much to be seen.

At the eastern end, the branch started at a junction just west of Percy Main station (NZ 333672). It was from Percy Main to Carville over this next section, through Willington Quay and Point Pleasant, that the first experimental electric service began in 1903.

Willington Quay station (NZ 324665) has disappeared under a housing development called Hadrian Village, the residents of which would have appreciated a rail service to Newcastle or the coast from the surviving Station Road. A signal box with a hipped roof adorned the down platform,

Percy Main, with an NER electric train passing through. (Lens of Sutton)

while an NER footbridge connected the platforms. Although passenger services lasted until the end, goods traffic ceased in October 1967. On the last day some wag chalked up a sign reading: 'No more waiting here after today'.

Point Pleasant (NZ 314664) was a late addition to the branch, officially opened at the start of 1902, although workmen had used it for some time before that. The down platform had a signal box and a simple wooden building for the waiting room and ticket office, while on the up side was an open waiting shelter, with a sloping roof that continued over the platform as an awning. The original standard NER iron lattice footbridge disappeared before closure. In looks and facilities, Point Pleasant never lived up to its name and yet it was one of the busiest stations on the line. It closed with the branch in July 1973, although goods traffic had ceased in October 1967. Commercial development is erasing much evidence of this station.

Point Pleasant did not live up to its name, but was one of the busiest stations on the line! (Stations UK)

Carville station (NZ 302662), which opened and closed with the branch, was built on a curve and had a more elaborate version of the standard single-storey, twin pavilion brick building on the down platform. Here was the generating plant that supplied the Tyneside electric system and a tall NER signal box. A row of railway cottages called Carville Station Cottages still stands where Hadrian Road becomes Buddle Street.

Carville was only 200 yards from Wallsend station on the N&NSR but it was the busiest station on the branch, probably due to its proximity to the shipyards. Unlike Wallsend, it had a big goods yard, partly for the coal traffic to the power station, and after December 1913 the yard here was known as Wallsend Goods, but it closed in July 1966. The old station house has become the Segedunum Business Centre, on the corner of Buddle Street and Station Street, which passes

The nearby shipyards and power station brought a great amount of business to Carville station. (Stations UK)

under a nice cast-iron over-bridge to Swan Hunter's shipyard.

Not much further on is Segedunum (Latin meaning 'strong fort'), the only place in the ancient Roman Empire where you can see a whole fort laid out. It was the base for 480 Roman infantry and 120 cavalry at the eastern end of Hadrian's Wall, a section of which is nearby (www.twmuseums.ogr.uk, www.hadrians-wall.org). The branch line ran between the fort and Swan Hunter's and is visible from Segedunum.

Within sight of the N&NSR until now, the Riverside Branch then turned southwest and followed the river for some way to Walker. A number of railway works can be seen between Carville and Walker. These include a large set of bridge abutments on the borough boundary between North Tyneside and the City of Newcastle and in Welbeck Road, as well as a small over-bridge in Mary's Place, a viaduct in

53

Mitchell Street by the Wincomblee Hotel and a steel girder bridge over White Street just before it joins Station Road. The Riverside Branch at this point has been converted into a walk called Hadrian's Way.

At Walker (NZ 296642), station walls and the entrance are visible although the site now belongs to a scrap merchant. The long-gone platforms were connected by a subway and there was a hipped roof signal box on the down platform. Walker, called Low Walker from May 1879 until May 1889, closed to passengers with the rest of the branch but goods services had ceased in August 1967. Between here and St Anthony's was a 300-yard tunnel.

St Anthony's (NZ 285631) was west of a three-arch viaduct, to the east of which are steps to the walkway and track bed. To the west was the station forecourt and main buildings.

The viaduct in Mitchel Street, on the line between Carville and Walker. (Author)

St Anthony's was the first station on the line to close, in 1960. (Stations UK)

Under the viaduct, at the river's edge, is the railway retaining wall. There were no freight facilities and the station, opened with the branch, predeceased its fellow stations in September 1960. The buildings, which were similar to those at St Peter's, had gone by 1963.

St Peter's (NZ 275637) used to have a single-storey, twin pavilion brick building on the down platform with a subway to connect the platforms, and was busy with workmen's trains serving, amongst others, Hawthorne Leslie's locomotive works. The goods yard closed in October 1966 but passengers were welcome until the closure of the branch. Because it was next to a scrap yard the line from St Peter's to Percy Main was kept open after closure, until September 1987. In 1961 HM The Queen Mother used the station on her way to launch a ship. 'Her' platform was decorated but a train hid the other undecorated one from the royal view!

The railway line turned away from the river, inland towards the N&NSR, at one point in a cutting between two roads with the trackbed visible from an over-bridge. It then passed through the sharply curved 140-yard Byker Tunnel (NZ 267646), which still exists under shops on Shields Road, to Byker station (NZ 264648), immediately east of the junction. Byker station was a late addition to the branch, officially opened in March 1901, although by then workmen had used it for some time. It closed in April 1954, having never been busy. The site has now been filled in.

The western end of the Riverside Branch was at a junction (NZ 264549), immediately west of Byker station, with the N&NSR east of Manors and west of Heaton, where the East Coast Main Line curves away to the north, some 220 yards past the eastern end of the 918 ft long x 108 ft high Ouseburn viaduct.

Workmen's trains kept St Peter's station busy. (Stations UK)

Byker station only opened in 1901 and was never particularly busy, closing in 1954. (Stations UK)

The Quayside Branch

This mile-long branch ran from Argyle Street on the East Coast Main Line immediately east of Manors station, through a steep, curving, U-shaped tunnel to Newcastle Quayside (NZ 259641), at gradients as steep as 1 in 27.

In 1905, following the electrification of the Tyneside lines, two Bo-Bo electric locomotives were built, using overhead and third-rail power supply at the same 600 volts DC. The overhead wires were at Argyle Street and at the exchange yard on the quay, and the third rail was in the tunnel. The changeover from pantograph to third-rail operation was done on the move and required two men, one to lower/raise and lock the pantograph and the other to operate the switches which connected/disconnected either the pantograph or the shoes. Good timing was essential, as changeover too early,

57

A steam train shunting on Newcastle Quayside, which has since been completely redeveloped. (Ken Hoole Collection)

before the third rail started, would mean no power, but too late and the pantograph would hit the tunnel mouth. Shunting on the quay was by 0-6-0 tank steam locomotives, but in 1964 diesel shunters replaced both electric and steam locos until the line closed in June 1969.

The site of the junction can no longer be discerned and the area of the quayside where the line emerged from the tunnel has been so comprehensively redeveloped that nothing remains of the line.

3

The Blyth and Tyne Railway

The B&TR Main Line
The Blyth Branch
The Avenue Branch
The Ashington & Newbiggin-by-the-Sea Branch
The City Branch
The 1882 NER Coast Diversion
Tyne Commissioners Quay
Stephenson Railway Museum

The Blyth and Tyne Railway (B&TR) was the last independent line between the Humber and the Tweed, running from Morpeth to Bedlington, where the branch from Newbiggin-by-the-Sea and Ashington joined, and on to Tynemouth and New Bridge Street in Newcastle. Although the name 'Blyth and Tyne' was first recorded in 1847, the B&TR was a private railway, not incorporated until 1853.

In June 1840 the Seghill Railway from Seghill Colliery to Northumberland Dock on the River Tyne opened, with passengers conveyed from Percy Main to Seghill from August 1841. By 1846 the line had reached Hartley and the Avenue Branch from Hartley to Dairy House had opened, from where a private line or waggonway ran to Seaton Sluice. The line was extended north of Hartley to Newsham and Cowpen Colliery by 1847, with Blyth reached in March. Thus the original 'main line' ran from Blyth to the Tyne at Percy Main via Hartley and Seghill. By late 1850 passenger and mineral

59

The B&TR platform at NER's Morpeth station in 1963. (R.K. Blencowe)

The Blyth and Tyne railway's first station at Morpeth photographed in 2005. (Author)

traffic had started from Bedlington Colliery to Newsham via Cowpen Lane.

Private railways like the B&TR paid wayleaves to landowners for each ton of coal passing over their land and in addition, the Inland Revenue refused to exempt private railways from the duty on passengers carried at under 1d per mile (as public companies were allowed). These financial burdens, and potential competition from other proposed lines, led to incorporation in 1853. A line from Newsham to Morpeth opened in October 1857 and from the following April the line to Morpeth became the 'main line' in place of that to Blyth, which became a branch.

In 1859 a branch was built from Bedlington to North Seaton, with a private line to North Seaton Colliery. The following year the Avenue Branch was extended from Dairy House Junction to Tynemouth via Monkseaton (where the branch from Backworth would later join), and Cullercoats, using the route of the Whitley Waggonway route at the southern end. The line from Monkseaton to Hotspur Place (Backworth) and thence on to Benton, South Gosforth and Newcastle New Bridge Street, opened in June 1864. In 1865 the original Tynemouth station was renamed North Shields when the branch was extended closer to Tynemouth, and by 1872 the line from North Seaton had been extended to Ashington and Newbiggin-by-the-Sea.

The B&TR, which had started as a glorified series of colliery waggonways, was by the early 1870s carrying a million passengers a year. Although its route from Tynemouth to Newcastle was longer, it charged the same as the North Eastern Railway (NER) and its carriages were some of the best in the land. It was also competing with the NER for the Morpeth traffic. From October 1864 the B&TR issued third class tickets on all its trains. Within six months the shareholders were reaping the benefits as the numbers travelling rose. By the 1870s it widely advertised its regular services as well as the many specials – to the theatre, races or shows and fairs. However, those convicted of not paying their fare or being drunk on the train were dealt with rigorously, and had their names and details of the offence and punishment publicly displayed. The fines could be quite heavy. In 1851 a first class ticket from Blyth to Newcastle cost 2 shillings but the fine for travelling without a ticket was 40s (£2)! In 1860 the stationmaster at Hartley was paid only £1 a week.

In the end, the NER could tolerate its little neighbour no longer and in 1874 it absorbed the B&TR. When, in 1882, the NER opened a new coast line nearer the sea from Monkseaton to Tynemouth, the old line was abandoned and the Avenue Branch closed.

In 1905 the B&TR line from New Bridge Street was electrified via the coast to Newcastle Central and in 1909 New Bridge Street station was closed and the line extended to Manors. Electric train services were extended from Manors to Newcastle Central in 1917. The electrified part of the B&TR is now an essential part of the Tyne and Wear Metro and the 'main line' from Backworth via Bedlington to Ashington and Morpeth is still in use for freight, although passenger services on the B&TR lines to Newbiggin, Bedlington, North Seaton, Bebside, Newsham, Blyth, Hartley, Seghill and Seaton Delaval ceased in November 1964. Services between Bedlington and Morpeth via Hepscott and Choppington had stopped in April 1950.

Luckily, a lot remains of this plucky little line.

The B&TR Main Line

The B&TR station (NZ 204854) opened in Morpeth in the summer of 1857, just south of the N&BR station. By July 1862 the Wansbeck Valley Railway (WVR) had also reached

Morpeth from Reedsmouth Junction and, having crossed over the N&BR track, joined the B&TR at an east-facing junction, so that WVR trains originally had to reverse into the B&TR terminus. In 1871 the WVR flyover was removed and a link built for the WVR to use one side of the island platform on the north of the NER station, while B&TR trains used a bay platform on the south. The B&TR Morpeth terminus became a goods station. Both the B&TR station and goods shed still survive.

All signs of Hepscott station (NZ 223845) have been erased, except for a small cottage where the line crosses the road. The down platform had a small stone building and an NER wooden shed served the up side. Choppington (NZ 256835) had a stone station building at right angles to the down platform by the level crossing but evidence of this is long gone.

All traces of Hepscott station have been erased, shown here in 1963. (Stations UK)

Choppington's stone station building, at right angles to the level crossing.
(Lens of Sutton)

Bedlington station (NZ 276830) was situated immediately south of the junction of the Morpeth and Ashington lines. Passenger traffic started in August 1850, even though the station was not ready until November. It only ever had one through platform, which served trains in both directions, plus a bay platform for the Newbiggin branch. Although services ceased in November 1964, the two signal boxes, platform, bay platform and the main station building still exist. Despite the glazed canopy and its supporting columns being no more, one can sense the atmosphere of this station in its heyday. Sir Daniel Gooch, Locomotive Superintendent of Isambard Kingdom Brunel's Great Western Railway when he was only 21, was born in Bedlington on 24th August 1816.

South of Bedlington the B&TR crossed the River Blyth, shortly after which came Bebside station, called Cowpen Lane until 1862 (NZ 283815). All traces have totally gone, except for a small wooden hut. Like Bedlington, this station

The one through platform at Bedlington station. (Lens of Sutton)

The viaduct that carried B&TR trains over the River Blyth. (Author)

was not ready until November 1850, but when completed had brick buildings on both platforms.

Newsham station (NZ 302796), the junction for Blyth, has also completely gone but level crossings remain on the lines to both Bedlington and Blyth. The main line at Newsham had two straight platforms, connected by a tiled subway that flooded in bad weather. The eastern one of these formed a south facing 'V' with the curved Blyth branch platform. It once had a stationmaster who was renowned for his very loud voice that could scare unwary patrons!

At Hartley (NZ 313769), the track divided, one line going south to Tynemouth along what became known as 'The Avenue' branch while the main line turned west towards Seaton Delaval. The main line and level crossing are still in place and the line of the Avenue Branch can be clearly seen. This station was like Newsham in plan, but the other way up, with the 'V' pointing north instead of south. Here the main

Only a small wooden hut remains to mark where Bebside station once stood. (Ken Hoole Collection)

Newsham station, where the subway connecting the platforms flooded after rain. The Blyth branch platform is on the right. (Lens of Sutton)

Seaton Delaval station, called Seaton Delaval Colliery until 1864. (Ken Hoole Collection)

67

line to Seghill was on a very tight curve and had check rails fitted throughout the station, and the single straight platform was for the Avenue Branch. The two-storey brick building that stood on the diverging platform is in private use and in the garden is part of the Avenue Branch embankment.

West of the level crossing is a public footpath alongside the line, a little way along which is a widened fenced area around the base of a small building. Seaton Delaval station (NZ 296758) was in a cutting where the road crossed and was called 'Seaton Delaval Colliery' until 1864. The new 1884 NER station had a booking office and waiting rooms on the bridge, while the two-storey stationmaster's house, with a porter's room, was on the down platform. This station has completely gone.

Seghill station (NZ 293745) now only has a single track line through the site, although when there was double track the down trains had to use a crossover to reach the single platform. This boasted a modest single-storey brick building, of which no sign is now visible. Holywell station (NZ 306723)

Signals at Seghill station. (Lens of Sutton)

also has nothing remaining, other than the track. It opened with the line and in 1860 was renamed Backworth, closing when the new Hotspur Place opened on the City branch.

The original line ran due south from here via Prospect Hill and Percy Main to the coal staithes at Northumberland Dock. Gradients of between 1 in 228 and 1 in 63 meant that much of that section was worked by stationary engines until cuttings were made. In 1864, when the City Branch opened, a junction was put in south of Holywell curving west to Backworth. Whereas the old main line through Prospect Hill is now closed, the Backworth to Holywell line is still open to freight.

The Blyth Branch

Because the harbour at Blyth was not deep enough for large ships, a line to the Tyne was a priority and the rails reached Blyth in March 1847. For a while this was the main line, but it became a branch in April 1858 after the Morpeth branch from Newsham opened. By 1961 Blyth had become Europe's busiest coal handling port.

Blyth's first station (NZ 312817) was in Croft (later King) Street. One February morning in 1861 the passengers on the 8 am train for Newcastle were waiting to leave when they were rocked by a huge explosion and showered in soot, steam and flying metal. The engine boiler had exploded! Parts were thrown up to 1,000 yards away and yet driver and fireman escaped with minor injuries.

In 1867 a larger station further west along the line was built. This was rebuilt in 1894-6 by the NER, with an island platform partly covered by a glazed roof.

Originally services to Blyth were from Percy Main via Seghill, and later from Tynemouth via Whitley, but after the opening of New Bridge Street in Newcastle services along the Avenue Branch from Monkseaton to Hartley ceased. Then,

Despite being a coal port, Blyth station handled many passengers. (R.K. Blencowe)

Blyth has had a station since 1847, which was essential to its development as the busiest coal-handling port in Europe. (R.K. Blencowe)

when the ex-B&TR lines from Newcastle via Benton to Monkseaton were electrified in 1904, services were reintroduced over this section. The LNER used Sentinel steam railcars on the Blyth to Newcastle service and the articulated *Phenomena* spent all its life working between Monkseaton, Blyth and Morpeth. In addition there was a Blyth to Morpeth service until the section north of Bedlington closed in 1950. In 1961 about 114,000 people used Blyth station, but still it closed to passengers in November 1964. The station was demolished in 1972 and replaced by a supermarket.

The Avenue Branch

The track of B&TR's Avenue Branch can be traced from Hartley via the gap in the trees, where it crosses the Avenue between Seaton Sluice and Seaton Delaval. Here was the Avenue Halt, which closed in 1864. The line ran parallel to the coast, passing the sites of the junctions of both the waggonway to Seaton Sluice at Dairy House (NZ 322753) and that of the ill-fated NER branch to Collywell Bay. Between 1851 and 1852 there was a passenger service of sorts from Seaton Sluice along the waggonway. Over a hundred years later, on the night of 28th October 1954, the Royal Train with HM Queen Elizabeth II and HRH Prince Philip on board parked there.

Whitley (NZ 347722) was the next station. In 1864 the New Bridge Street line joined the Avenue Branch and a new station was opened south of the level crossing over Marine Avenue. The up platform had a brick hipped roof building with round topped windows and a hipped roof canopy, while the eastern platform had a smaller building and the signal box. The first signalman ran this as a social club with a reading room and debating society, as well as providing the services of a hairdresser and selling sweets and refreshments.

In 1882 the NER built a new line nearer the coast which diverted from the B&TR line just south of Whitley station and that July the station was renamed Monkseaton to distinguish it from the new Whitley (later Whitley Bay) station on the coast line. The original B&TR line to Tynemouth, with the exception of the short length from the new line which was used as a headshunt to reach the 1860 B&TR Tynemouth station, which had become a coal depot, was closed.

In 1905 the line from New Bridge Street via Backworth was electrified and in July 1915 the NER opened a diversion, taking the line from Backworth through a new Monkseaton station (NZ 347721), with Marine Avenue crossing over the railway. At the same time the bottom of the Avenue Branch was realigned and the junction moved. The original Whitley station was closed and nothing remains (NZ 347722). The tennis courts in Souter Park are its approximate location.

A contemplative commuter at Whitley station! (Lens of Sutton)

Station Road, Whitley Bay in about 1910. (Stations UK)

NER electric trains at Backworth station. (Lens of Sutton)

The first Cullercoats station (NZ 356709) opened in June 1864 and closed in July 1882 when the new NER coast line opened. The site was used for a post-war housing estate and, although all indications that there was ever a station here have gone, some people can remember the disused platforms in a field.

When Cullercoats was a fishing harbour the fisherwives wore a traditional costume – because they helped with the boats they had skirts above their ankles and thus got a bad reputation! Having launched the boats, the fisherwives would carry their menfolk through the water to get on board, to keep the men's boots dry. While the men were out fishing, they gutted and prepared the fish and then travelled distances with their fish creels, often by train, to sell it. The arrival of electric trains caused problems for the Cullercoats fisherwives. They had been allowed to use any steam train with their fish but they were restricted to certain electric trains as the water from the fish made the carriages smell!

From Cullercoats the line continued south, along the eastern edge of what is now Northumberland Park to the original 1860 B&TR Tynemouth station on the north side of Tynemouth Road (NZ 364690). A temporary station was soon replaced with a brick building containing booking office, waiting room and first class ladies' room!

In 1865 a branch from just north of the 1860 station curved east under Mariners Lane to a new station (NZ 368693), approximately where the TA Centre is today. Despite the longer route to Newcastle, the B&TR charged the same fares as the NER, which lost 17,000 passengers in the first week. In 1864 and 1865, while this B&TR station was being built, a temporary terminus called Tynemouth was constructed just past the new junction. Once the 1865 station had been opened this was renamed North Shields and the old station became North Shields terminus! Nothing remains of either the 1865

Tynemouth or North Shields stations. The 1860 station became a coal depot, which lasted until May 1971 when the site was cleared and the buildings removed.

The 1882 NER coast line had a junction immediately south of the 1882 Tynemouth station. The 1882 main line cut across the B&TR line to the 1865 terminus while the other track took a sharp curve to the west to join the 1865 B&TR line under Mariners Lane to service a coal depot at the 1860 station. That cutting under Mariners Lane can still been seen.

The Ashington and Newbiggin-by-the-Sea Branch

In November 1859 the B&TR opened the branch from Bedlington to North Seaton, although the planned extension

The B&TR branch from Bedlington to North Seaton, shown here, opened in 1859. (Lens of Sutton)

to Warkworth was never built. Leaving the B&TR main line immediately north of Bedlington station (NZ 276830), it ran north via West Sleekburn (junction to Cambois), over the River Wansbeck on a viaduct, to North Seaton station (NZ 278862), a short way north. Only the signal cabin is left, the two-storey main building having gone.

The original viaduct was constructed from 1,200 tons of wood and was 400 yds long and 85 ft above the summer water level. It was the largest wooden structure in Britain.

Ashington station (NZ 273877) opened in 1878 as 'Hirst' until October 1899, but the original station buildings with a glass and wood frontage and glazed canopies have gone, leaving only the 572 ft long platforms. The junction (Newbiggin-by-the-Sea to the right) and signal box are visible from the north side of the road bridge. Ashington has been described as the largest pit village in the world and one of its claims to fame is that it was the birthplace of footballing legends Jack and Bobby Charlton.

Before reaching Newbiggin the branch served a number of pits, including what is now the Woodhorn Colliery Museum and Queen Elizabeth Country Park. There is a railway track from the colliery museum to the lake using a colliery locomotive - *Black Diamond*.

Newbiggin-by-the-Sea, a small Northumberland coastal village, had once been third only in importance to London and Hull for the shipping of corn, and latterly had become a fishing village, but during the 19th century it had grander aspirations of becoming a major seaside resort. This meant attracting a railway line. The 1872 branch ended a little way from the sea (NZ 309878), at a point shortly after the mineral line to Lynemouth branched off.

Because of the village's ambitions to become a popular beach resort, the station had an attractive H-shaped building, with Dutch gables surmounted with finials alongside the main platform. In 1904 the NER lengthened the platforms and the LNER later considered two different extension schemes but neither was implemented. Services from Blyth ceased in November 1964 and the tracks from Woodhorn to Newbiggin-by-the-Sea were removed. The station site was cleared in the mid 1970s and houses later built. The Railway Hotel is now the only visible reminder of the branch.

The City Branch

The B&TR's City link ran from the Avenue Branch at Whitley (later Monkseaton) to Hotspur Place, on to South Gosforth and into Newcastle, opening in June 1864.

Heading towards the city from Whitley, the first station was Holywell & Earsdon, followed by Hotspur Place shortly before the line to Percy Main crossed over. It was later replaced by Backworth, west of the junction with the line from Hartley. Backworth station building was brick and single-storey, with a canopy between two end pavilions, but from 1904 a wooden booking office was built on the road over the bridge. Backworth closed in June 1977 and was demolished within weeks. However, the Metro authorities have built a new station on the same site to serve the new Northumberland Park housing estate.

From Backworth to Jesmond, the B&TR route via South Gosforth is now used by the Tyne and Wear Metro, with all the B&TR stations except Jesmond, Forest Hall and Long Benton modified as Metro stations. Forest Hall (NZ 285694) was east of the N&BR line, while Long Benton (NZ 271686) was a little west of it, approximately where the present Four Lane Ends Metro station is situated. Both were open between June 1864 and January 1871, when Benton (NZ 277689) opened.

Jesmond (NZ 254654) was another of the original stations, then at the northern edge of built-up Newcastle, and consisted of a two-storey, gabled Gothic-style brick building,

An NER electric train at Jesmond in about 1910. (Newcastle City Libraries)

with stone facings and double side gables on the down platform. When the City Branch was converted into the Metro, the line was diverted into a tunnel north of, and under, the original station and there is still a single track for empty Metro stock. The station's platforms and waiting shelter survived and the station building has become a restaurant with a GNR teak dining car, initially in varnished teak livery with GNR markings, though by 2005 it had become a dull green colour.

The original Newcastle terminus of the B&TR was at New Bridge Street (NZ 253646), renamed Newcastle (New Bridge) after 1871, and designed by John Dobson, the architect of Newcastle Central station. Known as Picton House, it was an Italianate building with a hipped roof, entered from Picton Place, a curved street which met Oxford Street at New Bridge Street. It originally served only Tynemouth and Morpeth. How different it would have been if the NBR had bought the

B&TR and their expresses to Scotland had started there!

From 1904 the station had a new lease of life as the terminus for the electric services to Central station via the coast. When the NER absorbed the B&TR in 1874, a three-quarter mile link from New Bridge Street station to Manors was planned, but it was not built until January 1909. New Bridge Street closed then and passengers used an extension of Manors, called Manors North.

Initially, electric trains still ran only to Manors, but in March 1917 through services started from Newcastle Central station round the coastal loop. To build this line the Trafalgar goods shed had to be moved to New Bridge station, which became solely goods and remained in use until December 1967, despite being badly bombed in September 1941, during the Second World War. The A167 central motorway roundabout now occupies the western part of New Bridge

Dignitaries at New Bridge Street station on the day of its official opening. (Ken Hoole Collection)

79

Terminus and Picton Place. A quick glance as one is driving round the roundabout gives a glimpse of the trackbed.

The NER 1882 Coast Diversion

After acquiring the B&TR, the NER built a new line closer to the coast from just south of Whitley station (Monkseaton from 1882) to the N&NSR line at Tynemouth. This coastal loop opened in July 1882.

All the stations on that line survive but Whitley (NZ 358719), 'Whitley Bay' after July 1899, was rebuilt and moved in October 1911. The original 1882 station had been in what is now the forecourt of the 1911 station and had canopies over the platforms. From the forecourt in front of the new station you will notice that it is dated 1910, although all references to its opening are given as 1911. You can also see the original alignment of the track bed to the north and south, clearly defined by the trees and houses. Nearby is St Mary's island lighthouse, the last Trinity House light to be lit by paraffin (www.stmarys-lighthouse.ntb.org.uk), now a museum with shop and café, where you can climb the 137 steps to the lantern.

At Tynemouth a new eight-acre, eight-platform (for the tourist traffic) through station was built. The tracks continued south under Tynemouth Road to join the N&NSR towards Newcastle and create the coastal loop, the 1847 N&NSR station becoming a goods station. Now only two platforms remain in use, the others slowly decaying.

Tyne Commissioners Quay

The Tyne Improvement Commission, established by Act of Parliament in 1850, built a number of new quays with

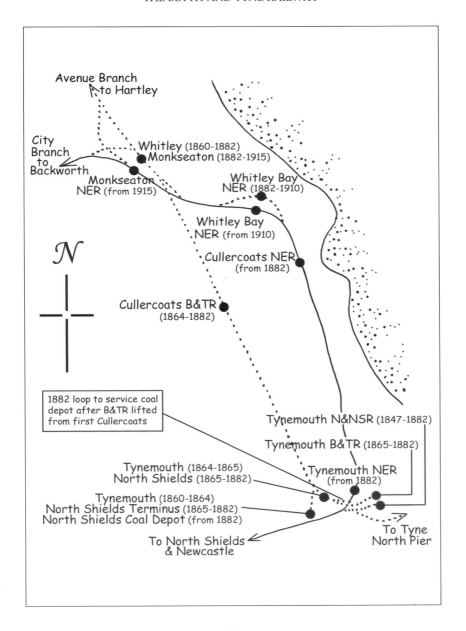

Avenue Branch
to Hartley

City
Branch
to
Backworth

Whitley (1860-1882)
Monkseaton (1882-1915)

Monkseaton
NER (from 1915)

Whitley Bay
NER (1882-1910)

Whitley Bay
NER (from 1910)

Cullercoats NER
(from 1882)

$\mathcal{N}$

Cullercoats B&TR
(1864-1882)

1882 loop to service coal
depot after B&TR lifted
from first Cullercoats

Tynemouth N&NSR (1847-1882)

Tynemouth B&TR (1865-1882)

Tynemouth (1864-1865)
North Shields (1865-1882)

Tynemouth NER
(from 1882)

Tynemouth (1860-1864)
North Shields Terminus (1865-1882)
North Shields Coal Depot (from 1882)

To Tyne
North Pier

To North Shields
& Newcastle

facilities for passenger ferries to Bergen and Oslo and a railway system to serve them, which began at a junction with the B&TR south of Percy Main. The LNER ran boat trains from Kings Cross, with four boat trains in each direction every day in the summer of 1938, before the Second World War.

From Newcastle, boat trains took the N&NSR to the junction with the B&TR west of Percy Main station, where there was a connecting curve with a B&TR station on it. Once on the B&TR, the engine ran round and pulled the train under the N&NSR line, going slowly around the tight curves to the passenger station at the quay. During the Second World War, the German invasion of Norway in 1940 brought these services to a halt, but they were resumed once hostilities had ceased. They became so popular that there was even a named train, the *Norseman*, from Kings Cross, which only stopped to pick up passengers at York and change engines at Newcastle. By the summer of 1959 there were 14 trains a week arriving and the same number departing. Through services to the Quay stopped in 1968 and the replacement DMU service from Newcastle Central only lasted until 1969.

Stephenson Railway Museum

The Stephenson Railway Museum in Middle Engine Lane, North Shields (www.twmuseums.org/uk/stephenson) is open daily, except Mondays and Fridays, from May to September, 11 am to 4 pm. Steam trains operate to Percy Main on Sundays and bank holidays, leaving the museum at 1 pm, 2 pm and 3 pm.

The museum is on the original B&TR main line between Percy Main and Seghill, south of Prospect Hill and where, much later, the new Metro rolling stock and equipment were tested. Here are great relics from the dawn of steam railways:

The North Tyneside Steam Railway operates trains from the Stephenson Railway Museum throughout the summer. (Author)

George Stephenson's *Billy*, a forerunner of the *Rocket* built before 1826; a Consett Iron Company engine of 1883 (one of the oldest working steam locomotives in the world); and an NER Electric Motor Parcels Van.

4
The North Northumberland Branches

Alnmouth to Coldstream via Alnwick
Alnwick to Coldstream: The Coldstream Branch
Berwick to Carham via Coldstream

Alnmouth to Coldstream via Alnwick

The Newcastle & Berwick Railway (N&BR) opened its branch to Alnwick, home of the dukes of Northumberland, in August

The Alnwick train at Alnmouth Junction in 1952. (R.K. Blencowe)

1850, starting on the East Coast Main Line at Bilton (NU 231110). This station was renamed Alnmouth after May 1892. The 'modernisation' of the 1970s left only the signal box, but the remains of the Alnwick branch platform can be found. The junction (NU 229115) was ½ mile north of the station.

The most startling event at the station came on Friday, 18th March 1910, when the 10.27 am from Newcastle Central pulled in at 12.08 pm. William Charlton, a porter, spotted blood in a compartment and made the grisly discovery of a body stuffed under the seat. John Innes Nisbett, who had been carrying the wages, amounting to £370 9s 6d, for the Stotswood Colliery Company, had been seen at Stannington but the compartment was empty at Morpeth, the next station. Nisbett had been shot in the head five times and his body hidden. The money was never found, but John Alexander Dickman was arrested and convicted of the murder. He was executed on 10th August 1910.

The original Alnwick station had a single platform with a stone, single-storey building containing offices and waiting rooms, a large stone goods warehouse and a signal box at the south end of the station yard. It was on the edge of the town at the end of a waggonway from the Shilbottle Colliery. The old station site is now a tyre depot.

In 1885 Alnwick council asked the NER for improved facilities and the present magnificent building and new signal box were built, in conjunction with the branch to Cornhill, both of which opened on 5th September 1887.

In 1911 there were 45 passenger trains a day between Alnwick and Alnmouth and three trains in each direction on the Cornhill branch. But by the 1920s road transport was taking business away, particularly on the Cornhill branch, which closed to passengers in September 1930. Trains to Alnmouth and beyond were reduced to fourteen each way, about half of which were through services to Newcastle or Berwick. In 1964 the branch was reduced to single track.

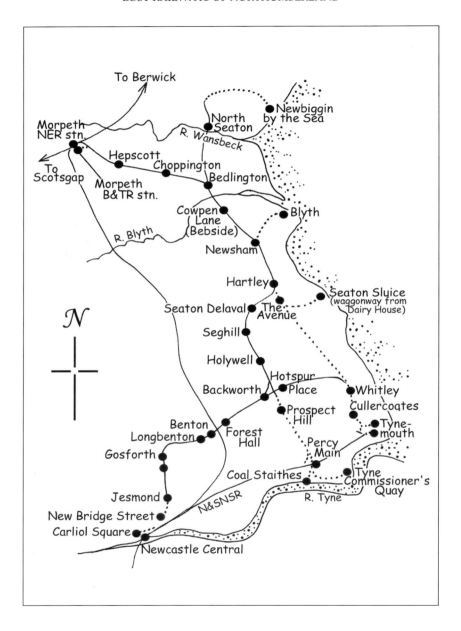

The 'new' Alnwick station in 1966. (R.K. Blencowe)

Alnmouth shed closed in June 1966 when the last steam passenger train ran, using 9F 2-10-0 No 92099 to mark the occasion. Diesel multiple units (DMUs) were then used until closure in 1968. The last passenger train left at 11.35 am on 29th January, bedecked with wreaths and supported by a large cheering crowd. Overseeing this last departure was Stationmaster Alfred Middleton, who was the eighth stationmaster since 1850.

After the closure the signal boxes, coal depot and weigh cabins were demolished but some buildings, including the goods shed, were rebuilt at Beamish Museum, County Durham. The 1887 station building remains largely intact, in exceptionally good condition and in use as a carpet warehouse and a secondhand book emporium, Barter Books. The bookshop is well worth a visit, filled with people browsing, drinking coffee and sitting in the old waiting room reading the books on offer.

The 1887 Alnwick station building, now a secondhand bookshop. (Author)

The Aln Valley Railway Society is working to rebuild and reopen the 3-mile line as a tourist railway.

Alnwick to Coldstream: The Coldstream Branch

The single track, 35¼ mile NER branch from Alnwick to Cornhill via Wooler was built to open up rural mid-Northumberland, something the NCR failed to do when it ceased to venture beyond Rothbury.

This branch is a delight as it had some of the finest station buildings ever provided on a rural line. However, the stations were a long way from the communities they served and with eight level crossings (controlled either from adjacent signal boxes or by crossing keepers who lived in line-side cottages), traffic was light, Even in 1911 there were only three passenger trains a day in each direction.

Even though passenger services ceased in September 1930, the LNER provided 'camping coaches' at a number of stations on the line, to which holidaymakers were taken in coaches attached to parcels trains. Floods in 1948 washed out a bridge south of Mindrum and the line became two dead-end branches, Alnwick to Kirknewton and Coldstream to Mindrum. The following year, floods destroyed another bridge between Wooler and Ilderton, so the Mindrum bridge was repaired and the line then operated from Alnwick to Ilderton until March 1953, and from Coldstream to Wooler until March 1965. There was no passing loop at Ilderton so, having reached there, trains had to be pushed back by their engine to Hedgeley where the engine could run round.

Avoiding the Duke of Northumberland's estate, the line swung south from Alnwick over difficult, sparsely populated

The viaduct and castle, close by Edlingham station. (Author)

terrain with sharp curves and gradients, before turning west towards Edlingham (NU 122093). This station had a single-storey building, with a glazed canopy between the two end pavilions adorning the single platform, and a separate station house. In 1926 it became a halt and the booking office closed. It is now a private house. The station, the five-arch viaduct (NU 117093) of roughly squared stone by the ruins of Edlingham Castle, and the embankment from the station to the viaduct can all be seen from the B6341. The viaduct, now a Grade II listed building, was shortly followed by the branch's only tunnel of 350 yards at Hillhead.

Next along this rural idyll was Whittingham station (NU 089121). It was the only one on the line with an island platform serving both tracks of the passing loop. A single-storey building had a glazed canopy all round which was supported on ornate brackets incorporating the Star of David. There was a signal box, goods shed, coal drops and a weigh-house. The unused goods shed and platform, devoid of glass

Whittingham station, the only one on this branch to have an island platform. (Lens of Sutton)

in the canopies, are still there amidst a small community consisting of the privately occupied station cottages and stationmaster's house.

Glanton station (NU 082148) was next and a little nearer the community it served than most on this line, which would have been useful for the annual Glanton Show which started in 1855. Now in private occupation, the single-platform station had the most common type of buildings on the line – a two-storey stationmaster's house and single-storey offices. Passengers waited for their trains in a wooden, glazed section in front of the building.

Hedgeley (NU 060170) was of similar construction. It was probably built for Hedgeley Hall, about a mile away, and for the stone crushing plant across the road from the station that ran a narrow gauge railway to a local quarry. A signal box controlled the passing loop and sidings and the line to the goods shed. The station is now a private house, while the goods shed in the yard is an antiques market. In the 1930s Hedgeley, and probably all the other stations on the line, had no electricity or piped water. The station house had an internal pump but the four station cottages shared just one outside pump.

Wooperton (NU 048201) was almost identical to Hedgeley, as was Ilderton (NU 019237). The latter is now a private house but has been used as a restaurant, with a short section of track and a coach.

On the south-eastern edge of the town, Wooler was probably the biggest intermediate station (NT 994285). The main building on the down platform had half-hipped roofs, an integral stationmaster's house and two waiting rooms, booking and luggage offices in the single-storey section. A glazed canopy covered half the width of the platform for the length of the building and there was a small glazed timber waiting room on the up platform. The platforms were linked by a footbridge. From 1936, except for the duration of the war,

91

A train leaving Ilderton station. (Ken Hoole Collection)

The station at Wooperton, which was almost identical to that at Hedgeley.
(Lens of Sutton)

the station was used as a Youth Hostels Association hostel, with one waiting room made into a women's dormitory while the other was for men.

The goods yard had four sidings, one of which went through a large stone-built goods shed, which still survives. Wooler also had two signal boxes, though the one at the south end of the station was only for the level crossing on Chatton Road. The buildings are now residential and commercial properties.

Leaving Wooler, the next station was Akeld (NT 957299), where we find the buildings, goods shed and weigh house in private use. This was another station with a signal box and a passing loop but only a single platform. The building was of the same design, but intermediate in size, to Wooler and Wooperton.

94

A few miles north of Akeld can be found the 15-inch gauge Heatherslaw Light Railway (www.ford-and-etal.co.uk), which runs from Heatherslaw Mill (NT 933383) to Etal Castle. Hourly steam services run from 11 am with extra diesel services at peak times, from late March to the end of October. Besides the railway there is a model railway exhibition, a working mill, café and shop, as well as other local craftsmen such as a working smithy and carpenters.

The next stop used to be Kirknewton (NT 910304), which was very similar to Edlingham. A single platform with a single-storey building was set hard against the road, with a glassed-in canopy between the two end pavilions. It is now a private residence.

Some 31½ miles from Alnwick was Mindrum (NT 855339), which served a very small community, another single-platform station with passing loop and the standard

Heatherslaw Light Railway runs steam trains from Heatherslaw Mill to Etal Castle. (Author)

Akeld, whose station building was similar in design to Wooler and Wooperton. (Lens of Sutton)

buildings. An old sign on the B6352 still points to Mindrum station along an unclassified road. A short way along is a small corrugated iron church, beyond which is the station with its fine example of an NER goods shed, set back from the road and in private use. Along the road are railway cottages and a road over-bridge to the north.

The line then headed for Cornhill on Tweed, on the outskirts joining the line from Carham to Berwick (NT 862388). Open from July 1849, but renamed Coldstream in October 1873, it closed to passengers in June 1964 and to freight in March 1965. The main building on the up platform consisted of a two-storey house and single-storey offices, while the other platform had a waiting room and porters' room. There was an NER footbridge and a water tower. It was approached down a carriage slope from the entrance of the now closed Station Garage. Nothing is left of the station (NT

Coldstream, originally named Cornhill on Tweed station. (Lens of Sutton)

863385) or the bridge that used to carry the line over the A697, although the abutments can still be seen. Just past the bridge is a turning to an estate of modern houses, although one terrace of older properties is named 'Station Cottages'.

Berwick to Carham via Coldstream

The N&BR were given the powers to build a branch from Tweedmouth to Kelso, which opened as far as Sprouston, 3½ miles inside Scotland, in July 1849. The two-mile gap between this line and the North British Railway (NBR) branch line from St Boswells to Kelso was bridged two years later when the companies met at Mellendean Farm.

Double tracked throughout, the line was little used for most of its life but became the hero of the hour after the floods of 12th August 1948. Six bridges on the East Coast Main Line (ECML) were washed away and the line was closed for about three months, so that the non-stop *Flying Scotsman* and other mainline traffic was diverted along this branch. In August 1954 the ECML was again affected by flooding and expresses once more used this line for a couple of days.

After those excitements the branch returned to its quiet ways and traffic slowly ebbed away. By July 1955 only Coldstream and Norham stations remained open for passengers and in 1962 the goods service was withdrawn from Twizell. In June 1964 passenger services ceased.

The branch left the ECML at Tweedmouth Junction (NU 994520), just north of Tweedmouth station. The first stop was Velvet Hall (NT 943491), a station named after a local house with the nearest village over a mile away. Open between July 1849 (as were the other stations on this route)

Nothing now remains of Tweedmouth, which closed to passengers in 1964. (R.K. Blencowe)

Velvet Hall was named after the local 'big house'. (Lens of Sutton)

and July 1955 (goods March 1965), the station had a two-storey house and offices on the Kelso platform and a waiting shelter on the other platform, with a signal box and goods shed. The station is now a private residence with the up platform, some gateposts and fragments of wall to be seen.

Norham station (NT 907468) closed in June 1964. Despair not, here the heart leaps, we have a treasure to behold! The station was on an embankment with the first floor of the station building serving the down platform. The up platform had a wooden waiting shelter and, after 1900, a signal box. There was also a goods shed. The welcome news is that all has been preserved by the former stationmaster and now houses a model railway as well as a large collection of both rail and non-rail ephemera, including the signal box, both platforms, goods shed, a lime depot, signals, assorted signs and lamps. Open Easter and bank holidays (other times by appointment, telephone 01289 38221), it is well worth a visit and run by a very friendly couple.

The history of this station typifies the way the rail authorities closed lines in the 1960s. Children used the trains from Norham to Tweedmouth to go to school. A simple change in the branch line timetable by three minutes meant that connections were missed and the children stopped using the trains. Before closure, the freight side at Norham had been profitable with large amounts of cattle, beet and potatoes being handled. Then BR's agent informed all the local farmers that the goods service would be discontinued within two months. As a result of the stationmaster's arguments his superiors relented, but by then it was too late, the six largest farmers, who accounted for the majority of the freight, had bought lorries. A year later the line closed.

The line continued its southwesterly progress to Twizell

Twizell viaduct, its six arches standing at 89 ft above the waters of the Till. (Author)

100

(NT 876437), named after the ruined castle – actually an 18th-century folly – and the ancient bridge at the confluence of the rivers Tweed and Till. It opened in August 1861 and closed to passengers in July 1955. The staggered platforms and unprepossessing collection of single-storey buildings have all gone, but you can walk along the track bed, which is now a footpath leading to Twizell viaduct, 133 yds long, with six arches 89 ft above the River Till. The short walk between banks of rosebay willow herb is worth it for the views.

After Cornhill on Tweed (described above), Sunilaws was the next station (NT 826374). It was originally named 'Wark' and renamed in August 1871. The station closed to passengers in July 1955 and to freight ten years later. It had staggered platforms either side of a level crossing, a two-storey combined house and office building on the up platform, a goods yard and a signal box. The station is now a private house, complete with Kelso-bound platform, NER

The track at the Sunilaws level crossing has been tarmacked over, but some parts still show through. (Stations UK)

101

clock, gateposts, goods dock and postbox. At the level crossing the track was tarmacked over, although bits still show through. Just east of Sunilaws the road goes under the line and shortly leads you to a fine bridge and good views of the trackbed.

The branch crossed the border (NT 794372) and the short length from Carham to Sprouston was the only English railway to reach into Scotland, although three of the five Scottish railways entered England. Just over the border was Carham station (NT 791371), open until July 1955 for passengers. This was very like Sunilaws with staggered platforms, and these are all that now remains, with the Kelso one an extension to the garden of a nearby house, planted with miniature shrubs.

The line continued to Sprouston station (NT 760353). A combined house and office on the up platform still exists as a private house, with a garden on part of the trackbed. This station served as the terminus of the line for two years until the connection to Kelso (NBR) was completed in 1851. Although the actual end-on junction with the NBR was 1 mile west, Sprouston was the NER's last station on the line, so it had a single-track engine shed for the engines used on the Kelso-Tweedmouth services. It was closed in 1916 but was used during the Second World War to house GWR's *City of Truro*, evacuated from the York Railway Museum.

In February 1911 the *Daily Mail* offered £1,000 for the best bunch of sweet peas grown by an amateur gardener. Sprouston's minister, Rev. Denholm Fraser, entered the competition. He was not well off, was married with a small family, but he wanted to built a chancel to his small kirk. His wife, too, wished she could afford to decorate and furnish the manse in a more comfortable way, especially for her growing family. The minister had only just taken up gardening and had grown his first sweet peas the previous year. Armed with the latest books, he and his gardener planned their campaign.

At the end of July 1911, when the blooms had to be cut and entered, there was a drought across the UK, except in Sprouston when rain fell at just the right time. On 25th July, Denholm Fraser cut two bunches of twelve blooms, one entry each for himself and his wife, and posted them the next day. By noon on 28th July, 38,000 bunches of flowers were received at a special marquee at the Crystal Palace. The Rev. Fraser won third prize, and his wife won first prize. That little kirk did get its chancel in 1912 and Mrs Fraser was able to make the manse more homely.

5
The Coastal Branches

The North Sunderland Light Railway
The Amble Branch
The Seaton Sluice or Collywell Bay Branch

The Newcastle & Berwick Railway (N&BR) opened in 1847 and became part of the North Eastern Railway (NER) in 1854. For most of its length it kept away from the sea and two of the coastal branches in this chapter (Amble and Seahouses) came off the East Coast Main Line, while the other was built by the NER from a Blyth & Tyne Railway (B&TR) line.

The North Sunderland Light Railway

North Sunderland, 8 miles southeast of Belford, has always been a fishing port and, following improvements to the facilities in 1889, it expanded so much that it could take up to 300 fishing vessels. For its harbour, the name Seahouses was used to avoid confusion with Sunderland in Durham, which was becoming a major shipbuilding port.

Poor roads gave problems getting the fish from the harbour to the N&BR station at Chathill. After the NER rejected requests for a branch line, local merchants and fishermen formed their own company and the 4-mile North Sunderland Light Railway (NSR) was authorised in 1892. Construction began in 1896 but the planned station at Fleetham was abandoned to cut costs. An extension to Bamburgh was mooted but this, like the promoters' idea of a new seaside resort of St Aidan's-on-the-Sea between Seahouses and Bamburgh, was never constructed.

This line, which opened in 1898, was an oddity as it was always independent and never part of the NER, LNER or BR. It closure only came about because, in latter years, it had to borrow locomotives from its neighbour and in 1951 BR ended that arrangement. The railway officially closed on 29th October 1951, though the last train had been the 4.20 pm from Seahouses on Saturday, 27th October. The company was not legally incorporated until April 1952, and then wound up in June 1952.

The NSR started at Chathill (NU 186270), which had opened in March 1847 as a wayside station on the East Coast Main Line. On the down platform the now Grade II listed building, with a two-storey bay corbelled out to support a gable, survives as a private house but electrification saw the removal of the NER footbridge and electric lighting

Chathill station, on the East Coast Main Line, was the start of the North Sunderland Light Railway. (Stations UK)

replacing oil, although one of the old lamp supports survives. The remains of the bay for NSR trains can be found on the far side of the up platform at the north end of the blue shelter.

Immediately north of the platform was a run-round loop for the locomotive before the line curved eastwards to run almost straight for the 4 miles to Seahouses, a journey which took 15 minutes. The line was almost level with a very few small earthworks, shallow cuttings and low embankments. One of the few cuttings and road-over bridges can be seen at West Fleetham (NU 192286).

North Sunderland station (NU 210316) originally had a single wooden platform on the southeast side of the track. At the Chathill end was a single siding on the northwest, entered from the Seahouses direction. Past the platform was a level

The surviving NSR platform shelter at Chathill. (Author)

crossing, next to which stood the station building, a small corrugated iron construction with a wooden lean-to awning. Set back from the track and separate from the platform, it was extended in 1901 so the train guard and his wife, who operated the level crossing, could live there. Goods services ceased in February 1928 but passengers were still welcome until the railway's closure in 1951. All that remains of the station is the platform retaining wall, built in yellow brick. The trackbed to Chathill is completely overgrown, but to Seahouses it is a public footpath.

The terminus, Seahouses (NU 219320), had a single platform on the northwest of the track, which ran past to a corrugated iron engine shed. In 1902 the curved metal roof was replaced with a pitched slate roof. Southeast of the platform road was a run-round loop and two sidings, one for

Seahouses station in 1958, a far cry from its busy heyday serving the port and mines. (Stations UK)

NER 'Y' Class train at Seahouses. (E.E. Smith)

fish and the other with coal pens, a crane and a corrugated iron warehouse, similar to the engine shed in its original condition. The pitched roofed, corrugated iron station building contained the stationmaster's office and the booking office, waiting room, parcels office and ladies' room, the recessed part designed so the roof formed an awning over the platform. The site of the former station is now the main car park for the village. A plaque commemorating the North Sunderland Light Railway has been put up and the only remaining indications of the station are the yellow bricks in the base of the wall, which were part of the platform.

The Amble Branch

Amble is a small harbour on the south side of the mouth of the River Coquet, from which coal was exported, first aided by waggonways and after 1849 by the 5¾ mile Amble branch line. Passengers were carried from February 1879 and, despite having to change trains at Chevington, business on the branch was good until the advent of motor buses after the First World War. Passenger traffic ceased in July 1930, although the goods service continued until the 1960s. The branch was closed in October 1969.

The branch left the East Coast Main line at Amble Junction (NZ 221984), about 1¼ miles north of Chevington station (NZ 222969), where a gantry signal box straddled the main line. From 1879 to 1930, Amble Branch passenger trains used the down side bay platform.

The line was almost level, with few shallow cuttings or low embankments, and was single track to Broomhill (NU

Broomhill station in 1910, the platform crowded with passengers. (Stations UK)

109

246012). This station opened in 1878 and had a single platform with a long wooden station building containing offices and waiting rooms on the down side of the line. Immediately northeast of the station, by the goods shed, the branch became double track to Amble. The site has been cleared since closure.

Amble station (NU 267045) opened when the passenger service started and had a single platform on the down side with a slate-roofed, two-storey brick structure with the first floor at platform level. The goods yard with shed was to the southwest of the platform. The double track continued past the station another 500 yards to the coal staithes, where it was crossed by the waggonway from Radcliffe and Hauxley collieries to Warkworth harbour. A number of collieries were served by branches and, in one case, an aerial ropeway. The site has been cleared and is now a landscaped grassy area used for walking dogs but the line of the railway, some old walls, where the line went on to the staithes and where the waggonway crossed it, can all be seen.

The Seaton Sluice or Collywell Bay Branch

Seaton Sluice, now a small village, was originally the two entirely separate settlements of Seaton Sluice and Old Hartley, the earliest records of which date from 1097.

Apart from the rivers Tyne and Tweed, there were no significant natural harbours along the Northumberland coastline and as the coal trade grew, so did the need for new ports. Seaton Sluice developed slowly, from a small natural harbour in 1565 to exporting glass and coal from the 30-odd pits in the district near Hartley township in the 18th century. Ships of up to 300 tons visited, and hundreds of seamen, miners and associated trades (ropemakers, sailmakers, shipbuilders) found employment here. Today, Seaton Sluice is a quiet resort and the once busy little harbour now has small fishing boats at the moorings.

Despite its long history as a port, the railway did not come to Seaton Sluice until the start of the 20th century, after the harbour had declined. The NER had seen the positive effects of the electrification of the coast line and thought that an electrified branch would encourage house building and commuters. To make it more attractive to potential housebuyers, the name Collywell Bay was chosen, rather than Seaton Sluice.

The NER had expected to start services in November 1914 but after the outbreak of the First World War house building ceased and the tracks meant for the line were taken for battlefield use. Later a single track was reinstated for a coastal defence gun mounted on a rail wagon.

The branch would have started at a junction (NZ 338736) with the Avenue Branch of the Blyth & Tyne Railway (B&TR), just before the line crossed the Briardene Burn about a mile north of Monkseaton (NZ 348721). The junction of the Avenue branch can be seen from the road bridge over the line north of the present Monkseaton station. The route of the branch is now a path and the Collywell Bay branch junction is identifiable, but from here to Briardene station the line has been swallowed by a golf club. It headed northeast towards what is now the A193 but never reached the road, turning north to run parallel with it.

West of where the A193 returns to its northerly route, having dog-legged round what is now the caravan park, was the only intermediate station, Briardene (NZ 340744). The bridge abutments at the site are still there, as is the embankment to the one remaining bridge abutment at Old Hartley, where the B1325 to Earsdon was crossed.

It was at the New Hartley Colliery that one of the greatest mining tragedies occurred in June 1862. Some 200 men and

Bridge abutments at Briardene, one of the few remaining relics of the branch line that never was. (Author)

boys, some only 11 or 12 years of age, died when a beam engine fell down the only shaft. Knowing rescue was hopeless, they lay down in rows to die, boys with their heads on their fathers' shoulders. Every house in Hartley lost someone. Sixty thousand people lined the four miles to Earsden churchyard, and Queen Victoria is said to have cried when she heard the news.

From the B1325 the line of the railway is covered by the housing that came too late to save the line, proceeding to Collywell Bay station (N Z336763), which was close to where the Seaton Burn curves to the sea.

In 1924 the LNER reviewed the project, but the tracks were lifted in the early 1930s so this branch never carried passengers. The irony is that today the site of Collywell Bay station is covered with houses and Seaton Sluice has grown dramatically, all of which could now have provided customers for the branch that never was.

6
The NBR in Northumberland

Hexham to Deadwater via Reedsmouth:
The Border Counties Line
Morpeth to Reedsmouth via Scotsgap
Scotsgap to Rothbury: The Rothbury Branch

The North British Railway (NBR), in its attempts to get independent access to Newcastle, controlled some 75 miles of railway and about 25 stations in Northumberland, all of which are now closed. However, there is still much to be found which will give the explorer a real sense of the atmosphere of these lines in the countryside.

Hexham to Deadwater via Reedsmouth: The Border Counties Line

On 11 December 1855 the first sod of the 26¼ mile Border Counties Railway (North Tyne Section) was ceremoniously cut and by April 1858 it had opened as far as Chollerford. The line was originally planned to run from Border Counties Junction, west of Hexham, to Belling Burn, near Falstone, but by December 1859, when trains had reached Countess Park, the company had Parliamentary agreement for it to meet up with the Border Union Railway (BUR) at Riccarton, producing a 42 mile single track railway.

Before this could happen, the NBR and BCR amalgamated,

in 1860. The whole line was operational by July 1862, although Deadwater station was not opened until 1880. The NBR had access from Border Counties Junction to Hexham and Newcastle on the condition that the NER was given access along their main line to Edinburgh Waverley from Berwick, something the NBR was to rue for many years. Every day the NBR ran a train from Duddingston in Edinburgh's brewery district to Newcastle Forth Banks over the BCR.

The Border Counties line ran through a sparsely populated area and by the mid 20th century it had been making a loss for many years. Flood damage to a bridge near Hexham was the final straw and led to the withdrawal of passenger services in October 1956. On the last day of public running most of the passenger trains carried wreaths. Goods traffic from Riccarton Junction to Bellingham and traffic between Reedsmouth and Border Counties Junction ceased in

Reedsmouth in its heyday, with a North British goods locomotive and the station staff posing. (Lens of Sutton)

September 1958, but the line seemed to be fighting back. While removing track from the Border Counties bridge, a crane fell into the Tyne!

Bellingham to Reedsmouth was kept open until November 1963 for freight, which reached the remainder of the railways system via the WVR, Reedsmouth to Morpeth line. There are occasional reports of plans to use part of the trackbed from Riccarton Junction to Kielder in the construction of a freight line to carry timber from Kielder Forest. This would depend on the partial reopening of the Border Union Railway to Riccarton Junction. Other press reports have suggested reopening the line from the south for Army access to its firing ranges, but so far nothing has happened.

The BCR left the NCR line at Border Counties Junction (NY 924652), west of Hexham. The signal box here also controlled the junction to the Hexham and Allendale Railway. The line then immediately crossed the Tyne ½ mile south of the meeting of the South and North Tyne rivers, on a skew four-span bridge, the pillars of which can be seen from the westbound A69.

From here the BCR followed the North Tyne River for almost its entire route. Only 3¼ miles from Hexham, we have our first exciting discovery, at Wall (NY 917684). This station consisted of a single platform with two single-storey stone buildings, with a short canopy between them. One of the stationmaster's daughters started a fire with an oil lamp in the attic that was so bad all that only the waiting room and the signal box survived – a wooden waiting shelter had to be provided for passengers and a camping coach for the stationmaster and his family.

Both passenger and goods services ceased here in September 1955 – only 138 tickets were sold in the whole of 1951! The exciting thing is that the station has been rebuilt, although with a paved rather than ash platform. Even more is to be discovered! The signal box and weighbridge hut remain

Wall, where the station has been rebuilt. (Author)

and have been joined by a BR Mark I Brake Corridor Second coach. The new owner is very friendly and welcoming.

At just under 5 miles along the line was Chollerford (NY 920705), which was renamed Humshaugh in August 1919. This station had a single platform with a two-storey, L-shaped house and a goods shed. A narrow gauge line ran to Brunton Quarry and a camping coach was provided in the final days of the line. The station closed with the branch and is now a private house with gardens on the trackbed. It has been planted so as to maximise the seclusion of the building from prying eyes! Here, in 1793, the British government made paper for counterfeit French money to destabilise the revolutionary French government.

Chollerton (NY 980719) came next and it, too, had a short single platform and a single-storey building, which had an enclosed, glazed central section. Later the NBR built a new and longer platform equipped with a wooden waiting shelter to the north, but still used the original building. The

116

Chollerford, renamed Humshaugh in 1919. (Lens of Sutton)

The old platform at Chollerton still survives. (Author)

117

later platform with its waiting shelter and lights is still there. The station closed with the branch and is now a private house.

Barrasford (NY 919736), close to a sizeable village and a ferry across the North Tyne River, had a two-storey building with arched doors and windows. It is now used by the Scouting Association as an Outward Bound venue. Besides the station building there is part of the platform and evidence of the level crossing with concrete gateposts, wood and rail fencing and a small wooden goods shed. Gunnerton Railway Circle members meet regularly at Gunnerton church, close to Barrasford.

At Wark (NY 871768), the two-storey building, both platforms and some outbuildings still exist as a private dwelling.

Between 1st December 1859 and 1st February 1961 there was a station at Countess Park (NY 869807), of which nothing

Barrasford station is used by the Scouting Association as an Outward Bound venue. (Lens of Sutton)

now remains. This was the last station before Reedsmouth Junction (NY 865820), some 15 miles from Hexham. Originally it was a simple affair with a passing loop and staggered platforms, but the opening of the Wansbeck Valley Railway east to Morpeth meant the station had to be rebuilt 100 yards to the south. The Riccarton to Hexham line had two platforms as the primary route and the Morpeth branch was provided with one.

The yard at Reedsmouth remained open after the rest of the BCR closed, as the Wansbeck route was used for freight to and from Bellingham. On the north side of the Riccarton line was a locomotive shed which was used during the Second World War to keep historic locomotives safe from bombing raids. The engine shed, all the platforms, the two buildings on the 'V' platform, the waiting shelter on the down BCR platform the station, and the signal box are all still there. The main buildings have been turned into private houses. Here

The buildings at Wark are now a private dwelling. (Lens of Sutton)

Reedsmouth Junction in 1956 – although situated at Redesmouth, the spelling of town and station are different! (R.K. Blencowe)

we have one of those little railway idiosyncrasies that simultaneously so delight and annoy us. Reedsmouth station is situated at Redesmouth. The spelling of the town and station are different!

The first station after the junction was Bellingham (NY 841833), or Bellingham North Tyne after 1948, where the railway and station were situated right in the centre of the village. When the line opened, Bellingham was quite an industrial centre with an ironworks. After closure the yard became a council roads depot, while the station building was used as council offices. On the platform is a wooden goods shed but the door has been replaced as the original is now an exhibit in the Heritage Centre. Schoolboys awaiting their train used to weigh themselves and write their weight on the door!

The Heritage Centre at Bellingham (www.bellingham-heritage.org.uk), a new building in the station yard, is the highlight of a visit here. One of its relics is a brass letterbox from the station house at Dalhousie, made from the locomotive that was pulling the train over the Tay bridge when it collapsed in 1879. The locomotive was retrieved from the seabed, ran for many more years, being known as *The Diver* or *The Dipper*, and was shedded at Reedsmouth for its final years after its midnight swim. Many hundreds of mementoes of this railway are preserved at the Centre, including scale models, maps and historic photographs of the line, stations, buildings, staff and traffic, as well as items ranging from tickets and signboards to railwaymen's lamps and tools and the original Bellingham station clock! The Heritage Centre is open Easter to October, every Thursday to Monday, 10.30 am to 4.30 pm. This is a 'must visit' location, so allow plenty of time!

Further north was Charlton (NY 811848), a small halt consisting of a short wooden platform and shelter, which closed in October 1862 and of which nothing remains. Next followed Tarset (NY 790853), which had a siding and a goods

Tarset station which also served as the local post office. (Lens of Sutton)

shed. It took its name from a ruined castle, the corner of which was destroyed in the building of the railway. The station was also the local post office. The single-storey, L-shaped building, having closed with the rest of the branch, is now a private dwelling, situated down a lane adorned with plenty of wooden gateposts and pieces of old rail.

Thorneyburn (NY 773864) was next, with the Thorneyburn Tileworks to the west of the station. This consisted of a single platform with a small wooden building that, for many years, only opened on a Tuesday. One of those moments of real excitement comes as you trace the line, because the level crossing is still here, complete. The gates are still closed against a train that will now never come. Even the wicket gates for the passengers still work and have their weights to close them.

Falstone (NY 726874) followed when one had steamed just over 25 miles along the branch. This single-platform station is still there, with its two-storey, L-shaped building in use as

The level crossing at Thorneyburn is still complete – a wonderful find for the railway enthusiast. (Author)

holiday lets. The stone signal box also survives. There was a mine at Falstone, which had its screening mechanism near the station, but there is now no trace of it. Because of the mountainous countryside and wild moorland around here, livestock farming was common, although coal mining was an important employer, as were local limestone quarries.

In 1862 the Plashetts Coal and Coke Company opened a drift mine by the Belling Burn and, with no road access, Plashetts station (NY 665902) was built to serve it. It had a single platform with a range of one-storey buildings on a raised platform, and a large water tank atop a two-storey building, all now beneath Kielder reservoir. In addition railway cottages, a public house and a church hall were provided. The colliery had cottages with a school, shop and chapel at Seldom Seen and a waggonway connected the mine with Plashetts station, where there were workshops, coke ovens, screens and a brickworks. By 1889 the Seldom Seen

124

The buildings at Falstone station are in use as holiday lets. (Lens of Sutton)

Plashetts station in 1912 – it now lies at the bottom of Kielder reservoir. (Lens of Sutton)

125

mine was closed, but two new mines were opened and Bank Top and Far Colliery villages built. During the general strike of 1926 the mine workings were damaged by flooding and in 1964 mining ceased. The bottom of the incline is now a pier used by the ferryboat service on the lake.

Lewiefield Halt (NY 646913), now usually underwater, had a wooden platform with two wooden buildings for the booking office and waiting room. It opened in 1936 for the nearby Ministry of Labour camp, at first for unemployed miners and shipyard workers, then as a home for conscientious objectors during the Second World War and finally for displaced people from Eastern Europe.

Next was Kielder station (NY 627935), the building of which is now a private house, situated beside Station Garage. The station was renamed Kielder Forest in 1948.

After the line closed the Kielder reservoir was constructed and much of the trackbed is below normal water levels. Embankment removal has erased other traces of its course. However, a very fine castellated viaduct near Kielder Castle still stands (NY 625935). This railway viaduct was built in sandstone in a 'baronial' style (featuring a castellated parapet and false arrow slits) to complement the architecture of the nearby 1st Duke of Northumberland's 1775 Kielder Castle, a Gothic-style shooting lodge. The viaduct has a span of 392 ft and rises 55 ft above the river. This is a rare example of a skew viaduct, whereby the arches are built at an angle. It is a Scheduled Ancient Monument.

From Kielder to Deadwater part of the old trackbed is in use as a cycleway, one of the leisure activities associated with the lake. Deadwater station (NY 603969) is now a private house, some way from the road. Deadwater opened on 1st March 1880 as a single platform station, adorned with a single-storey building. Passengers wishing to board the 6.55 am train had to notify to the stationmaster at Riccarton before 5 pm the previous day!

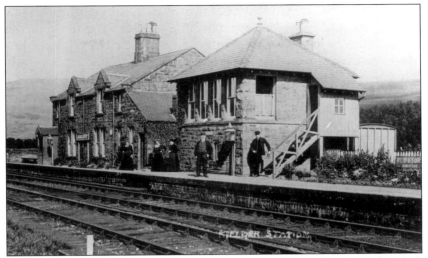

*Kielder station is now a private house. It was renamed Kielder Forest in 1948.
(Stations UK)*

Just past the station was a sign, now in York Railway Museum, denoting the English-Scottish border. The line continued, outside the scope of this book, to Slaughtree (almost 40 miles) and Riccarton Junction (42 miles), where the BCR joined the Border Union Railway.

Morpeth to Reedsmouth via Scotsgap

The Wansbeck Valley Railway (WVR) had opened in July 1862 as a single-track line from Reedsmouth Junction to Morpeth. In 1863 the WVR amalgamated with the North British Railway (NBR) and by May 1865 the branch was fully open to Reedsmouth.

The NBR at first saw the Wansbeck Valley Railway as

another means of gaining access to Newcastle, this time via the Blyth and Tyne Railway (B&TR) at Morpeth. That route was 13 miles longer than the NER line from Edinburgh to Newcastle, via Berwick, but it also meant gaining access to the port of Blyth. Hence the original plans for Reedsmouth Junction were for through running from Riccarton (and Edinburgh) to Morpeth.

However, by 1870 the NBR had their access to Newcastle, as we saw in earlier chapters. They still entered into discussions with the B&TR, but the NER sensed the danger and quickly bought the company in 1874, nipping the NBR's plans in the bud. As a result the line was not operated from Morpeth to Reedsmouth Junction and then on to Edinburgh, as originally intended, but from Morpeth to Rothbury via Scotsgap, with the Scotsgap branch to Reedsmouth being worked separately.

Passenger services were withdrawn in September 1952 and by November 1963 goods services had ceased beyond Woodburn. The last goods train ran on 29th September 1966 and a final excursion, the *Wansbeck Piper*, ran on 2nd October, with the line closing completely the following day.

From the north side of the island platform at Morpeth, NBR trains headed west towards Meldon (NZ 122834), a passing place with a single platform graced by a large two-storey building and signal box, with a separate stationmaster's house, sidings and goods shed. There are good views of what remains from the road over-bridge: the track bed is now a lawn and the station is private property.

Next was Angerton (NZ 088840), another passing place that had a level crossing. The station building was similar to that at Meldon but there was only a ground frame and no signal box. The station is now a private house with some bits of platform and goods dock remaining. The entrance to the goods yard was next to the level crossing and can be clearly seen by the gateposts.

Meldon, a private house with the old trackbed now a lawn, can be seen from the nearby road bridge. (Lens of Sutton)

Angerton station, with an NBR open wagon. (Lens of Sutton)

This was followed by Middleton (NZ 063852). The station was immediately west of the over-bridge east of the village but nothing remains of the platform or the small wooden building that once sat on it. The entrance slope to the station can be seen by the drive to a house called 'South View', planted with trees to disguise it.

Scotsgap (NZ 039864) was the junction for the NCR to Rothbury. This was where the trains were switched onto the correct track, and the two lines ran parallel to the actual junction (NY 034867) about ½ mile northwest of the station, where the tracks diverged left to Reedsmouth and right to Rothbury. The station was a single platform with a building like those at Meldon or Angerton, as well as a signal box, goods platform and goods shed. The old station building has been rebuilt and enlarged.

Trains from Morpeth went to Rothbury (see below) and the Scotsgap to Reedsmouth section was worked as a small

Nothing remains of the platform or wooden building at Middleton station. (Lens of Sutton)

Scotsgap was the junction for the NBR to Rothbury. (R.K. Blencowe)

branch, which sounded ecclesiastical with a Parsons Platform and a Vickers Platform – but the story behind those names will soon become clear!

Knowsgate station (NY 990858) had a single platform and single-storey stone station building, which still survives as a private house, with booking office and waiting rooms in an adjacent wood and glass building and a goods dock on the passing loop. The grassed platform, overgrown track bed, gateposts, sleepers and picket fencing can be seen. About a mile along the line had been a private platform for Sir Charles Parsons, whose country house was alongside the tracks. After his death in 1931 it continued to be used but had disappeared by the closure of the line. Between Knowsgate and Woodburn a number of collieries and quarries were connected with the mainline via tramways and 3 ft gauge railways.

The next station, Woodburn (NY 899860) had one platform, a single-storey building, a few sidings, a passing loop and a signal box. Troop trains used the station for a nearby military camp. The building is now a private house. In the 1890s the Newcastle and Gateshead Water Company created a reservoir at Catcleugh and built a 15-mile, 3 ft gauge railway north from Woodburn station using eight steam locos. This line operated for about a decade but there are few, if any, traces of it now.

About 3 miles further south was a halt called 'Vickers Platform' (NY 877837) and a south-facing junction to a line along the Broomhope Valley. Originally there had been ovens here to produce coke from local coal, needed to feed the iron ore blast furnaces. Imports killed that trade and the owners turned the valley into a firing range where the Vickers company tested their guns. Sir William Armstrong (later Lord Armstrong) was dissatisfied with the accuracy of British artillery used in the Crimean War (1854-1856) and

The signal box at Woodburn station. (R.K. Blencowe)

132

experimented with rifling field guns, as in small arms. His gun was 57 times more accurate than the current artillery. He gave the patent rights to the country and was knighted. During the First World War, over 10,000 guns were tested here, using 60,000 rounds of ammunition.

Scotsgap to Rothbury: The Rothbury Branch

In 1863 the Northumberland Central Railway Act authorised a line to be built from the Wansbeck Valley Railway (WVR) line, near Hartburn, to Ford with a branch to Coldstream (Cornhill) on the Berwick and Kelso Railway. However, the line was never continued beyond Rothbury so this was a 13-mile single track branch with intermediate stations at Rothley (Longwitton), Ewesley, Fontburn, and Brinkburn, which opened in October 1870.

In 1872 Rothbury engine shed, which had accommodation for two locomotives, was opened. This meant, after the amalgamation of the NBR with the Northumberland Central Railway (NCR), that services could soon run between Rothbury and Morpeth, with some through services to Newcastle. 'Race specials' to Rothbury races were popular and in the 1930s circular excursions, often using dining cars, were run from Newcastle to Rothbury, via Morpeth. After a stop for lunch, the return was via Scotsgap, Reedsmouth and Hexham.

This branch closed to passenger traffic in September 1952 and to goods in November 1963. The last train was a RCTS/SLS special, *Wansbeck Wanderer*, pulled by class 4MT 2-6-0, number 43129, on 9th November 1963. The track was lifted during mid-1964.

The branch left the WVR at Scotsgap Junction (NY 034867) and the first station was reached after 3¼ miles (NZ 045908).

Originally Rothley, a private halt for the Trevelyan Estate, in 1873 it became a public station called Longwitton. On 5th July 1875 there was a major accident south of Longwitton in which three people died and 25 were injured and the following year new facilities were provided at the station. It had a single-storey, clapboarded building with an old coach for storage. Nothing now remains except for a track with railway gateposts just south of the road over-bridge.

Ewesley (NZ 059927) was another station like Longwitton, with a brick stationmaster's house, goods siding, an old coach and goods dock. The house and some relics remain, but only the abutments of the road over-bridge are left. In the 1880s the NBR appointed a stationmistress for this isolated station.

The line then curved right and crossed the River Font on a stone viaduct consisting of twelve 30 ft arches, on its way to Fontburn (NZ 051942). In 1884 a siding for the Whitehouse limeworks was installed here, and in 1902

The Fontburn viaduct, with twelve 30 ft arches. (Author)

The station building at Brinkburn is now a private house. (Author)

another for the construction of a dam for Fontwell reservoir, when a number of 3 ft gauge lines were built between the station and works. Two years later Fontburn Halt opened to the public, with a single wooden platform and a very small wooden hut as a shelter.

Both Ewesley and Fontburn stations are far from obvious settlements that could have provided traffic for the line, but they did break the line up for signalling purposes, so that two trains could follow in the same direction. Access to Fontburn is impossible, but from the top of the dam (access NT 599929) good views of the viaduct can be obtained.

Brinkburn (NZ 088996) station building, which is now a private house, was similar to those at Longwitton and Ewesley, and there was a stationmaster's house and two small huts on the platform. There is still a road sign to 'Brinkburn Station' and the platform and station can be seen

135

from the new over-bridge at the south end. The Brinkburn Music Summer Festival is held in July in the beautiful Brinkburn Priory, an Augustinian foundation dating from about 1135 set in a loop of the River Coquet.

Finally, after 13 miles, the train would have reached Rothbury (NU 063017), the terminus of the line with a single 200-yard platform (long enough for the eight or nine-coach trains that ran on race days). The wooden station building was H-shaped, with the end of the platform covered by a canopy to shelter those using the normal two-coach trains. A turntable was placed at the very end of the line so that locomotives from arriving trains could continue onto it, be turned, and exit onto the run-round loop to get to the other end of the carriages for the return journey. There was quite a large goods yard here, and an engine shed. Today the station site is a car park and industrial estate. There are still (modern) animal pens by the former station's site.

Rothbury station in 1910, now a car park and industrial estate. (R.K. Blencowe)

Rothbury station in 1910, now a car park and industrial estate. (Stations UK)

Rothbury handled a lot of livestock for local farmers, most of which now goes by road. (R.K. Blencowe)

7

Lost Stations on Lines Still Open

The Newcastle & Carlisle Railway
The East Coast Main Line

The Newcastle & Carlisle Railway

In 1838, the last section of the Newcastle & Carlisle Railway (N&CR) line, between Greenhead and Haydon Bridge, was opened and through communication along the Tyne Valley, east to west, was at last possible by rail. The official opening was on 15th June at Redheugh. After the ceremony the guests crossed the river to Newcastle, but a collapsing walkway threw dozens of people into the river, including many ladies in light summer dresses. The N&CR's first trains had been leaving Carlisle from 6 am onwards, taking about four hours to reach the Redheugh terminus. At the conclusion of the day's events some 3,500 people from Newcastle took the round trip to Carlisle and back, many in open coaches. Not only did the return trip take over 16 hours, but heavy rain and fog were encountered and there was at least one accident!

After that inauspicious start the N&CR prospered. It was a go ahead concern and from its earliest days was a great innovator, for instance encouraging special kinds of traffic with reduced fares to markets, wrestling matches and horse races. It is believed to have been the first British railway to use handbills and posters to advertise its special offers and their agent at Milton, over the border in Cumbria, invented pre-printed tickets and a ticket dispenser.

Thomas Edmondson was born in 1792, one of twelve children. He had an inquisitive nature and as a teenager invented a machine for his mother which simultaneously rocked a cradle and churned butter. In 1836 he became stationmaster at Milton and was dismayed by the ticketing system, which was comprised of scraps of often illegibly handwritten paper. He started using cardboard for tickets and then made stamps to add the stations' names, the fare and a ticket number. Next he invented a rack that would hold the tickets in numerical order and drop them by gravity, so the next ticket could be pulled off the bottom. Because they were numbered, a daily check of the tickets indicated how many had been sold and thus how much money should be in the till. Then Edmondson invented his famous hinged machine for printing the date on the tickets. His machines, albeit modified over the years but using the same principles, were used from the late 1830s until the 1960s.

When first opened, and despite its name, the Newcastle and Carlisle Railway only reached Redheugh in Gateshead (NZ 246630), near the southern end of the present Redheugh Bridge. The original N&CR line from Redheugh via Blaydon to Wylam is outside the scope of this book as it followed the southern bank of the Tyne via Derwent Haugh. In 1904 the Dunston Branch, from Norwood Junction to Derwent Haugh and Blaydon via Dunston station, was built and the original route disappeared under Dunston power station. The junction (NZ187634) for the 1839 line over the Tyne to Scotswood was east of Blaydon station, which is open, although completely modernised. Also still open are Wylam, where the N&CR enters Northumberland, and Prudhoe. No longer do the Wednesday only 'hospital trains' run from Newcastle to Wylam. A flight of stairs linked the platform directly to the RVI convalescent home.

Stocksfield in its heyday. It is still open but unrecognisable as the same station. (R.K. Blencowe)

Mickley station (NZ 074629) opened in November 1859 but Mickley village was ¾ mile away and 300 ft above the railway. Low patronage meant that when a landslide in 1914 resulted in the realignment of the tracks, the station was not rebuilt.

The stations at Stocksfield, Riding Mill, Corbridge and Hexham are open. West of Riding Mill was Farnley Tunnel, one of only two on the line. In May 1962 the tunnel was closed and the line diverted into a new cutting to the south.

It is no surprise that nothing remains of Warden (NY 910661) and Allerwash. They opened with the first sections of the railway in the early 1830s but closed in 1837 and were replaced by Fourstones station (NY 889677), a single-storey stone station with bays on the platform side of the end pavilions, which closed in January 1967.

Haydon Bridge remains open. On 19th May 1857 the Prince of Wales, later Edward VII, stopped at this station. It is

A Freightliner Class 66 at Fourstones in 2005. (Author)

reported that he had wine and biscuits in the refreshment room and bought some books from the stationmaster's stall. One wonders what sort of books or wine the stationmaster of a minor wayside station would stock that might have been to the taste of the Prince of Wales!

Bardon Mill and Haltwhistle, junction for the Alston branch, are also still open. Shortly after Haltwhistle the line runs alongside the grounds of Blenkinsopp Hall which, up to about 1875, had its own private halt.

Greenhead station (NY 659654) closed in January 1967 and Gilsland station (NY 636663), named Rose Hill until 1869, is also closed. This was the last station on the line in Northumberland as the village of Gilsland straddles the Northumberland-Cumbria county boundary. Still there are the station building, the booking office and the

141

Gilsland station, known as Rose Hill until 1869, was the last station on the line in Northumberland. (Author)

stationmaster's house. From here, the N&CR passes outside the scope of this book.

The East Coast Main Line

The first services on the Newcastle and Berwick Railway (N&BR) started on 1st March 1847. The line is now part of the East Coast Main Line (ECML) with trains operated by GNER, Virgin Trains and Northern, but the only N&BR stations north of Newcastle which are still open are at Cramlington, Morpeth, Pegswood, Acklington, Alnmouth, Chathill and Berwick-upon-Tweed. Little Mill, Christon Bank, Newham, Lucker and Scremerston were closed between 5th May 1941 and 7th October 1946 as a wartime measure. However, September 1958 was a bad month for stations on the ECML. Forest Hall, Killingworth, Annitsford, Plessey, Stannington, Chevington, Warkworth, Little Mill, Christon Bank, Newham and Goswick were all closed on the same day.

Manors station was ½ mile east of Newcastle Central and opened on 1st July 1847, to be rebuilt after the line between Central station and Heaton was quadrupled in 1887. Once the electric services were brought south from the B&TR New Bridge Street station, Manors was extended with new platforms and a new entrance facing Carliol Square. This new part was known as 'Manors North' to distinguish it from the original, by then 'Manors East'. A big and busy station, Manors had nine platforms: 1 and 2 for Newcastle to the coast via Jesmond; 3, 4 and 5 for Ashington and Newbiggin trains; 6 and 7 for the East Coast Main Line and trains for Alnwick or Berwick; while 8 and 9 were for the coast via Wallsend and the Riverside line.

A train working hard at Pegswood. (Lens of Sutton)

Newham station, now a distant memory. (Lens of Sutton)

Manors in 1930, a big and busy station. (Stations UK)

144

By the 1960s Diesel Multiple Units (DMUs) operated the Blyth, Ashington and Newbiggin service and diesel locomotives were gradually replacing steam on main line services. The Riverside electrics ceased to run in July 1963, while the last electric train from Central station on the coast circle left at 6.15 pm on 17th June 1967. DMUs provided the service for a while but ceased for the conversion of much of that circle into the Metro. Trains to the coast via Benton were ended in January 1978, while trains to the coast via Wallsend ceased in August 1980. A business park now occupies the site of Manors North.

Gravity and the uphill gradient between Manors and Jesmond were sometimes used to transfer parcels vans into the bay platform, number 5. An engine would take a parcels van about 100 yards up the slope and stop. The van would be uncoupled and the brake released, allowing the van to run down the gradient into platform 5. Application of the brakes just in time to bring it to a halt as near to the buffers as possible required an experienced railman riding the van!

At Heaton Junction (NZ 274654), the ECML leaves the Newcastle & North Shields Railway (N&NSR). On 11th August 1974 the station was closed and within four months all traces of it had gone.

From here north, most of the N&BR stations were Tudor/Jacobean in style, built of stone with stone ornaments, and designed by Benjamin Green, who was also responsible for Grey's Monument and the Theatre Royal in Newcastle.

Forest Hall (NZ 277697) opened in 1856 (named 'Benton' until December 1874) and was demolished in 1964. The site of the station is occupied by the Flying Scotsman public house. The road now goes over a bridge but a metal gatepost of the old level crossing still exists. A signal box was placed high up on steel legs and an NER footbridge stood by the crossing.

The A4 Commonwealth of Australia at Heaton Junction in 1953. (E.E. Smith)

The NER footbridge at Forest Hall station in 1959 – the site is now occupied by the Flying Scotsman public house. (Stations UK)

The next two stations were Killingworth (NZ 268709) and Annitsford (NZ 257736). Both have closed, unable to compete with buses and trams. Killingworth had one of the original stone station buildings and an NER footbridge. Annitsford opened in 1878, but now only the steps up the embankment survive – because the line was on an embankment, the station building had one storey level with the road and an upper storey at platform level.

From 1805 to 1823 George Stephenson lived at Killingworth. Dial Cottage (NZ 275704) originally consisted of a ground floor with a ladder to a garret, but he converted it into a four-room house with a garden where he could grow prize-winning vegetables. In 1812 he was appointed enginewright at the colliery and his salary rose to £100 a year. He built sixteen locomotives while he worked at Killingworth and in 1821 he was employed to build the

Dial Cottage, George Stephenson's house at Killingworth. (Author)

Stockton & Darlington Railway. Modern rail transportation is considered to have started on 27th September 1825 when Stephenson's *Locomotion* ran from Darlington to Stockton, carrying 450 people at 15 miles per hour. Stephenson later designed and built the *Rocket*, which won the competition to find the fastest locomotive by travelling at an average speed of 36 miles per hour from Liverpool to Manchester in 1829. The *Rocket* ended its life on Lord Carlisle's Railway from Brampton to Lambley. George Stephenson died in 1848 and is buried at Holy Trinity church, Chesterfield. His equally capable son Robert, with whom he worked very closely, died only eleven years later in 1859 and is buried in Westminster Abbey, near to Thomas Telford. It is said that Robert was left-handed because, after his mother died, his father would hold Robert in his left arm while he read technical books with his right hand. Hence, young Robert's right arm was trapped and became the weaker.

Cramlington station is still open but Plessey (NZ 236784), which opened in 1852, is closed. Netherton (NZ 218815) station was renamed Stannington from January 1892 but only the L-shaped station building survives as a private house. Morpeth and Pegswood stations are still open.

Longhirst station (NZ 239894) closed to passengers in October 1951, and the station building is a private house. Widdrington is still open. Chevington station (NZ 222969) opened in October 1870 and between 1879 and 1930 Amble Branch passenger trains used the down side bay platform. The platforms have gone and the station building is a private house, while a siding with an old buffer stop and a loading dock covered in rosebay willow herb also remain.

Acklington station is still open. Warkworth (NU 233067) had one of the larger Benjamin Green buildings with three storeys, complete with a wide, splendid and impressive flight of steps to the entrance. It is now private property. All signs of the staggered platforms and subway are long gone.

148

Warkworth station had a three-storey building designed by Benjamin Green and reached by an impressive flight of steps. (Author)

After Alnmouth station, still open, came Lesbury (NU 229123), a small station only open between the opening of the line and 1851. Longhoughton station (NU 240149) is closed and nothing is left. Little Mill (NU 228177) was originally a private halt for Lord Grey of Howick, appearing in the timetable in 1861. On 27th September 1849 Queen Victoria had used the halt on her way to stay at Howick Hall before opening the High Level bridge in Newcastle. Now there is no sign of it.

Christon Bank (NU 213231) served passengers for 111 years and had a typical building for the line and a matching goods shed, both of which are in use as private residences, although the platforms have gone. Fallodon station (NU 209239) resembled that at Little Mill and was built for Sir George Grey of Fallodon Hall. The station remained private and in 1934 the

149

GNER 225 passing Christon Bank in 2005. (Author)

heirs of Sir George agreed to cancel their rights to stop trains in exchange for first class LNER all-station passes! One side of the level crossing is a large layby and parts of walls survive, leading from the road to the site of the station and backing on to where the platform would have been.

Moving north along the ECML, after Chathill the next nine stations are all now closed. Newham (NU 173282) has a modern house on the site of the station. Lucker (NU 153310) closed in February 1953, with the station being flattened in 1960. In 1898 the NER had installed water troughs south of the station to allow engines to pick up water without stopping. They were 1,869 ft long and 6 ins deep, and a train travelling at 60 to 70mph would collect 2,000 gallons of water in 20 seconds. There were five other sets of water troughs between London and Edinburgh on the East Coast route.

Falloden station, like Little Mill, was built as a private halt for the local landowner, in this case Sir George Grey of Falloden Hall. (Lens of Sutton)

Belford (NU 126336) was a substantial and elaborate station building, with the main entrance from the road having a three-arched portico. Opened with the line, it closed in January 1968 and the station building, which is now Grade II listed, is in private use. The mail coach *Royal William* passed through Belford each day until its last journey four days after the opening of the Newcastle to Berwick Railway in 1847. Why the *Royal William* and other coaches went out of business is obvious – they carried only a few people and were slow and expensive. Another coach, *The Lord Wellington*, in 1836 took 31 hours to travel from London to Newcastle and a further 6½ hours to Berwick. From Belford, Berwick was 1½ hours away but it took 5 hours to reach Newcastle. In 1842 the Royal Mail coach from Edinburgh to Glasgow charged 15 shillings to ride inside and 10s 6d

Belford station closed in January 1968. (R.K. Blencowe)

GNER 125 passing all that remains of Lucker station. (Author)

outside, whereas the Edinburgh & Glasgow Railway was charging 8s first class, 6s second class and 4s third class, all inside and much quicker.

Cragg Mill (NU 116349) was only open between February 1871 and September 1877, yet its elaborate buildings lasted until the 1970s and the brick-built station house survives. Smeafield (NU 093380) also opened in February 1871 but closed in May 1930. It only had a small station building, which has survived.

Beal (NU 062427) was once a popular station for visitors to Holy Island but, having been given a new coat of paint in 1967, it closed to passengers in January 1968 and all traces of the station have gone. Goswick (NU 046459) opened in November 1870 as 'Wind Mill Hill' with a staggered platform, but was renamed in January 1898. The station cottage and some walling remain. Scremerston (NU 021495) opened with the line and boasted a station rather like that at Widdrington,

Smeafield station opened in 1871 and closed in 1930. (Stations UK)

Beal station gave passengers access to Holy Island until 1968. (Lens of Sutton)

The station cottage remains from Goswick station, seen here in 1958. (Stations UK)

which still survives without platforms. In 1950 only £5 worth of tickets were sold and it closed in July 1951.

Shortly before Berwick was Tweedmouth Junction, where the line to Coldstream and Cornhill-on-Tweed left the ECML. Tweedmouth (NT 996519) was the end of the line from Newcastle until the Royal Border Bridge opened. A very large and lavish station, it was provided with a five-arched entrance mounted by Dutch gables and a hotel at the northern end. Originally a train shed covered the four running tracks and when these were removed in 1907, glazed awnings were provided over the platforms. An engine shed stabled some 50 locomotives in its heyday. The station closed with the Kelso branch in June 1964 and the fine buildings were all demolished. The site is now an industrial estate.

When the railways first reached Berwick in 1846, the 2,160 ft long Royal Border Bridge was not ready and road carriages conveyed passengers to meet the waiting York & Newcastle Railway trains. Forty minutes was allowed for this. In October 1848 passenger trains started to cross the Royal Border Bridge and on 29 August 1850 it was formally opened by Queen Victoria. The engine that pulled the Sovereign's train from Berwick to Edinburgh had been repainted in Royal Stewart tartan.

However, the problems were not over. The 1707 Act of Union had not abolished the frontier for 'colonial liquors' and Scotch whisky was so classified by the English Customs. The NBR posted notices warning its passengers that Customs officials would confiscate any whisky they considered more than reasonable for a traveller's personal refreshment. As can be imagined, what a Scotsman thought was a normal amount for his personal refreshment was greatly in excess of what the English Customs considered reasonable. The NBR complained to the government about the Customs delaying trains with their searches, while the Customs complained that

Tweedmouth, photographed in 1966, was a large and lavishly built station, the last stop before the Royal Border Bridge. (R.K. Blencowe)

the NBR was placing obstacles in the way of them doing their duty. Eventually the law was changed.

Berwick-upon-Tweed station still exists and is an important stop on the ECML. Berwick changed hands between the Scots and English 14 times before it was granted the status of a free town in 1482, which it remained until the Reform Act of 1885. When war was declared on Russia in 1854, it was in the name of 'Victoria, Queen of Great Britain, Ireland and Berwick upon Tweed and all British Dominions'. In 1856, when the Crimean War ended, there was no mention of Berwick in the Paris peace treaty. Thus Berwick was technically at war with Russia until 1966, when Russian officials made a goodwill visit.

Bibliography

A Regional History of the Railways of Great Britain, Vol 4, The North East, Ken Hoole

The Alston Branch, Stanley C. Jenkins

Border Country Branch Line Album, Neil Caplan

Border Railway Portfolio, Bill Peacock

The Blyth and Tyne Railway, Vols 1 & 2, J.A. Wells

British Railways Past and Present, No 4 The North East, Peter J. Robinson & Ken Groundwater

Exploring the Tyne Valley by Train, Rosemary Burton

Forgotten Railways, Vol 1, North East England, Ken Hoole

Memories of the LNER in Rural Northumberland, editions 1 & 2, Allan W. Stobbs

North East Branch Lines Past and Present, Ken Hoole

The North Eastern Electrics, Ken Hoole

The North Eastern Railway, Cecil J. Allen

Passengers No More, G. Daniels & L. Dench

Railway Stations of the North East, Ken Hoole

Railway History in Pictures: North East England, Ken Hoole

Railways in Northumberland, Alan Young

Roads and Rails of Tyne & Wear, J. Joyce

Suburban Railways of Tyneside, Alan Young

INDEX

158